The First Breakfast

MORNING, THE SEA OF GALILEE

The First Breakfast

A Journey with Jesus and Peter
through Calling, Brokenness, and Restoration

Eric and Kristin Hill

Photography by Hannah Elizabeth Taylor

W/M

With You Ministries Publishing

Printed in the United States of America.
Library of Congress Control Number 2019910760
ISBN 9780578544236

For our three beautiful daughters.

You always inspire us to search for beauty and truth.
Thank you for taking this journey with us.

TRADITIONAL CHALLAH BREAD

PROLOGUE
FOLLOW THE BREADCRUMB TRAIL

Take a good look at God's wonders—they'll take your breath away.

(Psalm 66:5 MSG)

"*Come and see what God has done.*" If your soul needs to remember, if you need to see the heart of the Father again, come and journey through the story of Jesus and Peter. If you've ever found yourself feeling weary, battered, or broken, discouraged, disappointed, or disqualified, come and see what God has done. His love for you stretches further than your mind can imagine. And there is rest for your weary soul.

His Covenant is greater than your commitment. The relationship between Jesus and Peter shows us that. God is the author of the greatest story ever told, and His heart beats for rescue, redemption, and restoration. God's Word has the power to transform us, to open our eyes to see who He really is and who we really are in Him. The living Word of God can reach into our lives today and pastor our souls, right where we are. Our hope is that, as we read through the true story of Jesus and Peter as it unfolds in Scripture, we can learn more about Jesus and who we are in His eyes.

The relationship between Jesus and Peter is an incredible picture of the Father's relationship with us. We can see ourselves in Peter. And when we look at the way Jesus pursues Peter—even in his brokenness—we can see more clearly God's pursuit of us and how we too, can be transformed by His redeeming love.

The apostle Peter is a well-known and well-developed figure in Scripture. He is bold and passionate, and although he is widely considered the leader of the disciples and the first New Testament Church, he is often remembered for his inadequacies. The story of Jesus and Peter is full of ups and downs, and there are so many times when Peter gets it wrong. But Jesus, with His great love, grace, and kindness, is there every step of the way, transforming Peter into who he will become.

And that's the reason we need to read this story. It can be easy to believe in transformation and restoration for other people. It's much harder to look within ourselves and believe that Jesus is doing the deep work of transforming and restoring us in our own day to day lives. But when we look at Peter, we often see something that feels familiar. Scripture opens our eyes to see that with God's Covenant Love, Jesus pursues Peter, even in his brokenness. Even when he gets it wrong. And when we see the way Peter's transformation unfolds, we just might be able to recognize the hand of Jesus reaching out to do the same for us. We just might be able to believe that He is restoring us, too, right where we are.

So many of us are longing. We are hungry. Our souls are starving. And here is the good news—*We have the opportunity to be filled.* Jesus is the Bread of Life. He is our daily bread. He alone can fill our deepest hunger and answer our deepest longing.

Throughout our journey together, we'll be following the breadcrumb trail that Jesus leaves for Peter. The words of Jesus call Peter back to Him, and as we read them in Scripture, we'll see that they're calling us, too. We can follow that same breadcrumb trail back to the Father.

God has always found a way to call His people back to Him. In the Old Testament, God parted the Red Sea to rescue His people and set them free. Moses led them from slavery towards the Promised Land. Exodus 16 describes their journey through the wilderness, and how God heard their longings and provided what they needed most. When they were hungry, "He gave them bread to the full, in the morning." That same chapter goes on to tells us that "when the Israelites saw it, they said to each other, 'what is it?' for they did not know what it was." Moses told them, "It is the bread the Lord has given you to eat." "The house of Israel named it *manna*," which literally means, "*what is it?*"[1]

So, together as we follow the breadcrumb trail that Jesus leaves for us, at every step of the journey we want to posture our hearts to ask the Lord that same question the Israelites asked: "*What is it?*"

Jesus, what is it that You have for me today? What is it that You want me to learn? Or maybe even un-learn? What is it that You want me to remember all over again today?" As we look to the heart of Jesus through His relationship with Peter, we remember, receive, and rest in God's heart for us.

These stories in His Word—these breadcrumbs—they are not scraps that have fallen from the table. They are not mere leftovers. They are part of the very Bread of Life—Jesus Himself—and He offers them to us to fill our deepest hunger. These breadcrumbs lead us on the path back to the true heart of Jesus.

And the invitation given to us each day is this—*Taste and See. Come and Follow.*

So as we begin this journey together, this is our prayer. We pray that spending time in God's Word—in the very presence of Jesus—will transform us, just as we see it transform Peter. We pray that we'll follow the breadcrumb trail that leads back to the Father's heart. We pray that we'll begin to see ourselves through the eyes of Jesus. We pray that we'll each have the courage to ask deep questions, to wrestle, to reach deep below what is happening on the surface and pay attention to what God is stirring in us.

A life-changing experience awaits us. Let's travel on this journey together, with Jesus and Peter through calling, brokenness, and restoration. The gift of a life lived from a place of true rest, and full restoration is waiting on the other side.

Please feel free to go at your own pace. Travel this journey as you feel led. For each step along the way, you'll see stunning photographs from deeply significant locations across the Holy Land. These beautiful images are a window through which we can see the actual places Jesus walked with Peter and the other disciples. The places where He preached the good news of the gospel, performed miracles, shepherded His followers, and made a way for all of us, back to the heart of God.

As you read the passages of Scripture, imagine what it would have been like to walk with Jesus, to be in His presence, and hear His voice. These passages follow the story of Jesus and Peter, but the living and active Word of God also reaches into our own lives today, just as much. If you find yourself wanting to engage with the passages of Scripture more deeply as you read, consider asking and answering the questions written below as you reflect.

Read, pray, study, ponder the truth in God's Word, and write in your journal or the blank space provided. Take on the posture of the psalmist who prayed in Psalm 139, "Search me, O God." And in that same way, position yourself to listen to the Lord and pay attention to what He is stirring up in you as you follow the breadcrumb trail that He is leaving just for you, right where you are today.

What is Christ stirring in me as I read this?

What is it He wants me to learn or remember again today?

What does this mean and why does it matter?

What do I see more clearly about Jesus from this passage?

What can I learn from Peter in this encounter?

What do I learn about the heart of Jesus by the way He relates to Peter?

What is the condition of my soul today?

Where am I right now, and what do I seek?

What are the ways that I see Jesus transforming me on this journey?

SUNRISE AT THE SEA OF GALILEE

INTRODUCTION

[1]After these things Jesus manifested Himself again to the disciples at the Sea of Tiberias, and He manifested Himself in this way. [2]Simon Peter, and Thomas called Didymus, and Nathanael of Cana in Galilee, and the sons of Zebedee, and two others of His disciples were together. [3]Simon Peter said to them, "I am going fishing." They said to him, "We will also come with you." They went out and got into the boat; and that night they caught nothing.

[4]But when the day was now breaking, Jesus stood on the beach; yet the disciples did not know that it was Jesus. [5]So Jesus said to them, "Children, you do not have any fish, do you?" They answered Him, "No." [6]And He said to them, "Cast the net on the right-hand side of the boat and you will find a catch." So they cast, and then they were not able to haul it in because of the great number of fish. [7]Therefore that disciple whom Jesus loved said to Peter, "It is the Lord." So when Simon Peter heard that it was the Lord, he put his outer garment on (for he was stripped for work), and threw himself into the sea. [8]But the other disciples came in the little boat, for they were not far from the land, but about one hundred yards away, dragging the net full of fish.

[9]So when they got out on the land, they saw a charcoal fire already laid and fish placed on it, and bread. [10]Jesus said to them, "Bring some of the fish which you have now caught." [11]Simon Peter went up and drew the net to land, full of large fish, a hundred and fifty-three; and although there were so many, the net was not torn.

[12]Jesus said to them, "Come and have breakfast."

John 21: 1-12 (NASB)

And so it was…The First Breakfast. After three years together, it wasn't the first invitation Jesus gave to Peter, but in so many ways, it was the most life-changing. *"Come and have breakfast…"*

The pastel morning sky painted the backdrop over the pebbled beach. The waves at the shore of the Sea of Galilee swayed back and forth, steady like a heartbeat. The crackle of the fire floated over the water. The breeze was fresh with the aroma of the sea and a breakfast of fish and bread.

The early morning sun would soon rise up out of the hills in the distance, beckoning not just a new day, but new mercies brought to life by the very sound of His voice. "Come and have breakfast." They don't sound like the kinds of words that could change a life forever. It's an everyday, ordinary sort of invitation. You might have even uttered those words yourself, standing bleary-eyed in your kitchen, this morning.

But on this unforgettable morning, the air became full with the life-altering possibility of redemption. Like when a storm rolls in, the air changed, the wind shifted, and the dark pebbled beach became sacred holy ground. This was no ordinary invitation to breakfast.

Burned in Peter's memory, were all the things that came to pass on the night of *The Last Supper.* Memories of denial, shame, guilt, inadequacy, fear, and regret. But this morning, filled with its new mercies and an invitation to redemption…this would become *The First Breakfast.*

Those words from Jesus—*"Come and have breakfast—"* became a melody to drown out the shame and regret. This invitation was a single moment, suspended in time, intentionally crafted by an all-knowing Savior, whose heart beats for restoration.

After three years, this moment is the crescendo in the life-changing story of Jesus and Peter. With all its sights, and sounds and smells, it paints the picture of how the saving love of Jesus covers over paralyzing shame, heartbreaking inadequacy, and the messiness of human brokenness.

It is the story of the reckless love of a Savior, chasing after an imperfect, flailing, believer. It is the story of Jesus and Peter. But it is, just as much, *the story of us.*

You and I. We too have felt the pursuit of His love and the gracious hand of His forgiveness. But we've also known the heartbreaking regret of our own mistakes, the pain of our own sin, and the brokenness of not measuring up. So, this sweeping cinematic story of the ever-turning, winding relationship of Jesus and Peter, we need to take it in. We need to climb to its highest heights and descend to its lowest depths. We need to see it in all its glory so that we'll understand the mysterious way the love of Jesus somehow covers over everything.

This story of Jesus and Peter—it gives us such an accurate picture of the infinite grace of our rescuing Redeemer. And it helps us to understand how He chooses and chases after the messy and broken ones He loves. And perhaps even more importantly, it teaches us *who we are* in the eyes of a Savior who emptied out His whole life for our very own. The words Jesus spoke to Peter on the beach that day were a simple invitation that changed everything.

They are a song of redemption—

For Peter.

For you.

For all of us.

This journey of Jesus and Peter is a true story. The question is, of course, *has it become true for you?* Can you see yourself the way Jesus sees you? Are you willing to take the journey that leads to being transformed by His presence? Will you answer the invitation He gives you each day to "Come and have breakfast?"

Like so many of the world's favorite stories, to truly appreciate the fullness of *the ending*, you have to go back *to the beginning.* To truly appreciate the fullness of God's promise, you have to go back and remember where the journey began…

SHORE AT THE SEA OF GALILEE

1

¹⁸Now as Jesus was walking by the Sea of Galilee, He saw two brothers, Simon who was called Peter, and Andrew his brother, casting a net into the sea; for they were fishermen.

¹⁹And He said to them, "Follow Me, and I will make you fishers of men."

²⁰Immediately they left their nets and followed Him.

Matthew 4:18-20 (NASB)

Our journey through the story of Jesus and Peter begins in the very place it will also end—*The pebbled shores of the iconic Sea of Galilee.* Almost all of the significant moments in Peter's relationship with Jesus will have their home near this water, its shores, and the villages nearby. The sights, the smells, the sounds—they will be the backdrop as their time together winds its full circle from beginning to end.

If this were a movie, the opening scene would be a sweeping shot of the lulling waves, panning out to reveal the dark, pebbled beach cradling a line of wooden fishing boats on the shore. Circles of fishermen are counting and weighing their daily bounty as children play under the shade of the trees lining the rocky beach. This is a snapshot of life at the water's edge by the Sea of Galilee. Rabbis of ancient times said, "The Lord has created seven seas, but the Sea of Galilee is his delight."[1]

The Sea of Galilee is today, just as it was also then—not really a "sea" at all, but actually, a freshwater lake surrounded by land on all sides. It's fed by nearby mountains and springs that combine at the head of the Jordan River to the north before passing through the lake. The Sea itself is actually quite large, measuring about 13 miles long and 8 miles wide. It's cradled low between hills and mountains, sitting 686 feet *below* sea level, making it the lowest freshwater lake in the world.[2]

According to the Gospels, Jesus' earthly ministry centered around the Sea of Galilee. Scripture sometimes uses the names "the Sea of Gennesaret" or "the Sea of Tiberius" to describe the Sea of Galilee, as well. While important events occurred in Jerusalem, Jesus spent most of His three years of public ministry along the shore of this freshwater lake. Here He gave more than half of His parables. And He performed most of His miracles here, as well.[3] The area was home to a variety of people, from religious zealots to pagans, from the devout to secular Jews. And on these shores, Jesus brought His life-changing message to them all.[4]

Scripture and the prophet Isaiah had foretold of the great awakening that would one day happen in Galilee, and for the people of God, that time had come. Isaiah 9:1-2 had already painted this picture.

> [1]"…Later on He shall make it glorious, by the way of the sea, on the other side of Jordan, Galilee of the Gentiles. [2]The people who were sitting in darkness saw a great Light, And those who were sitting in the land and shadow of death, Upon them a Light dawned."

The long-awaited Messiah and Light of the World had come. And now, He was shining His light on the Sea of Galilee. And that's where we begin our journey—on the beautiful shores of the Sea of Galilee. At first glance, everything about this story seems unlikely. It begins and ends in an unlikely place, and, as we'll soon read, the cast of supporting characters is made up of unlikely players. But everything about God's great redemption story is unexpected. And reading the story of Jesus and His relationship with Peter can help us better understand how we, ourselves, fit in the story of God's redemption.

At the end of his life, Peter—the Rock—will be a much different man than Simon—the fisherman on the day he meets Jesus. Three years following Jesus changes everything about the man Simon Peter had always been. The presence of Jesus truly transforms him.

The shores of the Sea of Galilee are sprinkled with small pebbles, stones, and rocks, creating a strikingly significant and poignant backdrop for our journey. Maybe you've been to a seashore and picked up a smooth stone. Maybe you've held in your own hands a rock that has been transformed over a lifetime on the seashore. It's a process called *weathering*—the process by which a rock is smoothed and changed by the gradual force of water over time.[5]

Ironically, this process of weathering is a pretty accurate description of the transformation that Simon Peter undergoes to become the Rock that Jesus knew He could become. A lifetime of being shaped by the Living Water—it's the very picture of the long and winding road of spiritual formation. It's a portrait of the way *a lifetime in the presence of Jesus is the most transforming force the world has ever known.*

And this is the reason we need to read the story of Jesus and Peter. It sparks hope in us, as we too, find ourselves in the messy middle of transformation. Jesus pursues Peter from the first day He calls him at the Sea of Galilee, to their last day on those same shores, and every day in between. Peter's journey isn't a tidy, linear, upward arc from beginning to end. Peter's journey following Jesus is up and down, and two steps forward, one step back. The only constant is that Jesus is there every step of the way, transforming Peter with His presence.

This story of Jesus and Peter, and the journey through calling, brokenness, and restoration, is also the story of how Jesus can transform each of us. *The messy middle of transformation takes a lifetime.* And Jesus meets us where we are, and day after day, His presence with us smooths the surface, softens the edges, and changes everything about who we are.

It is His constant presence *with us* that is the very thing that transforms us into who we will become. Wherever it is that you find yourself today, there is hope in the journey *because Jesus is with you.*

ISRAEL OVERLOOK

2

³⁵ Again the next day John was standing with two of his disciples, ³⁶ and he looked at Jesus as He walked, and said, "Behold, the Lamb of God!" ³⁷ The two disciples heard him speak, and they followed Jesus.

³⁸ And Jesus turned and saw them following, and said to them, "What do you seek?" They said to Him, "Rabbi (which translated means Teacher), where are You staying?"

³⁹ He said to them, "Come, and you will see." So they came and saw where He was staying; and they stayed with Him that day, for it was about the tenth hour.

⁴⁰ One of the two who heard John speak and followed Him, was Andrew, Simon Peter's brother. ⁴¹ He found first his own brother Simon and said to him, "We have found the Messiah" (which translated means Christ).

John 1:35-41 (NASB)

The prophet Jeremiah long ago said, "You will seek me and find me when you seek me with all your heart. I will be found by you," declares the LORD..."[1] And in these days, the people of God had long been categorized, not by their seeking hearts, but by the amount of religious training they'd received. In a system built on the shoulders of law and legalism, no one was looking for the Kingdom of God to break open right in the middle of all those fishermen, hauling their nets.

But that's the way of Jesus, isn't it? The King of Kings who chose to be born of an unmarried teenage girl, among the sheep and the cows, also chose to spend the first thirty years of His life, quietly working in the trade of His own father. Right from the start, this King's Kingdom was built upside-down. This Messiah would be nothing that the people of God expected, but in every way, exactly what their souls needed. And in the true way of Jesus, when He sensed the Father telling Him it was time to gather His followers, He literally walked the opposite direction of where all the bright, young, promising religious men were gathered in the temples. When it was time to find men who would leave everything they'd ever known and follow Him, Jesus looked right past those with pedigree and position and set His eyes on these ordinary men after God's own heart.

And before the day that Jesus formally calls the disciples to follow Him on the shores of the Sea of Galilee, Scripture gives us a glimpse into this earlier first meeting that would make that day possible. John the Baptist had prepared the way. He'd spent time in the surrounding regions, preaching far outside the temple walls to the faith-filled ordinary people about a man who would come after him—a man that would be everything the prophets foretold. John the Baptist had garnered many followers himself along the way, and among them were two sets of fishermen brothers who'd been hearing about the long-awaited Messiah who would come to rescue the people of God. Little did they know that their time learning from John the Baptist was positioning them to meet this Messiah themselves.

These two sets of brothers have followed their fathers' footsteps right onto the shores of Galilee and into their fishing boats. The first set of brothers is Andrew and Simon Peter. And the others are James and John. Having grown up in Jewish households, both sets of brothers would have received religious training as young boys. It was a common Jewish practice that the best students were encouraged to continue their study with a rabbi. Gifted students approached a rabbi and asked, "May I follow you?" In effect, saying, "Do I have what it takes to be like you?" The rabbi either accepted the student as a disciple or sent him away to pursue a trade.[2] So, the fact that these brothers have become fishermen means that they'd been passed over and missed out on the prestigious opportunity to continue their religious training.

So now, these brothers have become business partners. They spend their days fishing and have settled in a seashore village in Galilee, not far from where they grew up. But they've also become followers of John the Baptist. So while the path for continued formal religious training had been closed to them, their hearts were seeking, open, and ready when Jesus positions Himself to be found by them.

Andrew and another disciple hear John the Baptist calling Jesus "*the Lamb of God*," so they follow Jesus closely to hear more. Scripture tells us that when Jesus turns and sees them following, He does something characteristic of a rabbi, and something we'll see Jesus do over and over again. *He asks a question.*

God's been doing that since the very beginning of time, even though He knows the answers to *all* the questions that have ever been dreamed up, *ever*. In the Garden, God asked Adam and Eve, "*where are you?*" And it isn't because He "lost them" and needed help to figure out where they were. His question was of course, as it always is, to draw out what is stirring deep in the hearts of the ones He loves.

This very first meeting is no different. Jesus asks a question, not because He doesn't know the answer, but because in having these fishermen answer a question, He reveals what's really going on inside of their hearts. Jesus asks the two fishermen, "*what do you seek?*" They respond with a question of their own—"*Where are you staying?*"

At first glance, it might seem like they are making small talk by asking where Jesus is staying. But what these fishermen actually mean is something along the lines of, "Can we come along wherever you are going so we can hear more from You?" If this did end up being the Messiah they'd been waiting for, the brothers wanted to come and sit at His feet awhile. And by asking His question, Jesus gives them the opportunity to identify the true longing deep in their hearts. They want to know more, to see more, to discover for themselves, to be close enough to hear this man Jesus and what He has to say.

And Jesus then gives them a life-changing invitation to "*come and see.*" After spending time with Jesus, Andrew displays an incredible act of brotherly love. He goes to get his brother Simon Peter, so he too can meet Jesus.

The lives of these fishermen are about to be changed forever. But no one had any idea of the incredible depth and ripple effect that would occur, because Andrew, after meeting Jesus, also chooses to invite his brother into that moment as well. So much of our history in the family of God…so much of what we know as believers…even books of the very Bibles on our own shelves today have been influenced so profoundly, because of the way that Andrew invites Simon Peter *into this moment*, *bringing him to Jesus.*

So, the stage is set, and the cast of characters has been introduced. And for the first time, Jesus meets the men who would be His brothers until the end. For generations, the world has marked time by using the distinction, "Before Christ" and after. And this day—this meeting right here— was the mark on the timeline of their lives, and the day their souls would be changed forever.

So, today, as we begin this journey together, let's begin by reflecting on these questions from the heart of God…

Where are you?

And what do you seek?

And hear Jesus say to you today, "*Come and see….*"

PATH TOWARD GALILEE

3

[40] One of the two who heard John speak and followed Him, was Andrew, Simon Peter's brother.
[41] He found first his own brother Simon and said to him, "We have found the Messiah" (which translated means Christ).

[42] He brought him to Jesus. Jesus looked at him and said, "You are Simon the son of John; you shall be called Cephas" (which is translated Peter).

John 1:40-42 (NASB)

They say you never get a second chance to make a first impression. But what do they say if you find yourself standing face to face, looking into the eyes of God? This is no ordinary introduction, but then again, *meeting Jesus for the first time never is.*

Andrew had met Jesus first and then goes to get his brother Simon Peter, so he too can meet the Messiah. With what must have been complete anticipation, Simon Peter approaches Jesus—this man that the Scriptures talked about. This man they had waited for their whole lives. If on the way over, Simon Peter had been wondering what Jesus would be like, and what Jesus might say, he'd never have come up with the scenario that would soon follow.

> **Jesus looked at him and said, "You are Simon the son of John; you shall be called Cephas" (which is translated, Peter).**

If there is a list somewhere of the mysteries of following Christ, the introduction between Jesus and Peter has to be at the top of the list. At first glance, their interaction seems a bit strange, but in reality, it is actually quite profound. Once again, it's the upside-down way of Jesus. Because He is both God and man, Jesus doesn't see things merely as they currently *are*, but also as they *will be*. Maybe it's like when we put filters over our photos. The original image is still there underneath, but also somehow at the same time, the filter over it, turns it into something new.

Until this moment, Simon Peter had only ever been, *Simon*. He was an ordinary man with a common name who was working as a fisherman near where he grew up. We know from Scripture that he was married, his mother-in-law lived with his family, and he might have perhaps even had children. But up until this point, there is not much indication that he has yet done *anything to* earn the reputation of being anything other than Simple Simon, the fisherman.

But Jesus, of course, sees things not as they are, *but as they can be.* And in that moment, Jesus meets Simon, and can already see who he truly is…*"Peter."*

In the ways of the Kingdom of Jesus, it's not what we do, but who we are in Him, that makes us who we are. And right from their very first meeting, the "with-ness" of Jesus is already changing who Simon Peter is, and who he will become.

The Greek translation of the word used here in verse 42 where it says, "Jesus looked at him" comes from the original Greek verb *emblépō.* The word used here means "to look upon, to see clearly," or to "look with a 'locked-in gaze,' in a sustained, concentrated way, with special interest, love or concern."[1] "Jesus looked upon him with that divine glance which read the heart."[2]

The fact that this particular word is used here for the way that Jesus looks at Simon Peter in their first meeting is truly significant. *This is the first breadcrumb in the long trail of all the ways that Jesus pursues Peter's heart, always drawing him back to Himself.* With eyes that truly see into his soul, the message Jesus is sending to Simon Peter is this— "when I look at you, what I see is not who you are now, but who you are becoming in Me."

Someone once asked Michelangelo about his work carving a slab of stone. Michelangelo's response was, "I saw the angel in the marble and carved until I set him free."[3] In the same way, Jesus, with His deep and fixed gaze, looks at Simon Peter, calling out who he will one day become. Jesus speaks over Simon Peter a prophetic promise that is based, not on anything that Simon Peter has done, but is instead rooted in who he will become *in* Christ. In speaking the words to Simon Peter, it's as if Jesus is already making the way for His New Covenant. The way of the Old Law had taken many hearts captive, but the heart of Jesus sets the captives free. The heart of His New Covenant beats with a new message of hope, grace, and freedom, declaring over us…

"It's not in your *doing* for Me, that makes you who you are, but in your *being* in Me. *My Covenant with you is greater than your commitment to Me.* It will never be about what you've done. It will always be about who I Am. And it's ok if you don't see it yet… I do. And it's *because of who I am, that you become who you really are."*

The paradigm shift here is significant, not just for Simon Peter, but for each of us, as well. In the gaze of Jesus, the way He sees us is not determined by how we show up, or our reputation, or what we do *for* Him. He sees us through the filter of His own Covenant with us, and that makes everything look different.

And the most freeing thing is the way Jesus just speaks it out. He doesn't really explain or even expect Simon Peter to understand it all in that moment. His message is simply, "I know this is who you've always been, but this is who I see you to be, and it's because of who I am, that you become who you really are." It's how it is for Simon Peter. And it's the same for each of us today.

Jesus tells us who we are. All that we've ever done, all that we'll ever do, all the names or titles we've ever held, all the hopes and dreams we have set deep inside our hearts—they all pale in comparison to who Jesus says we already are. Who Jesus tells us we are *is the most important thing about us.*

That is a lot to get from one first meeting, but just as it is for Simon Peter, it is for each of us. *Jesus changes everything.* This foundational concept sets the tone for the entire relationship between Jesus and Peter, and in our relationship with Him, as well. We are already fully known in Christ. There is no need to strive, to try to measure up, or in the same way, hide or self-protect. He is initiating and extending a Covenant with us, that is based on who He is and what He has already done. And because of that, freedom and rest are available to our souls today.

His Covenant with us is greater than our commitment to Him, and what a freeing place to start.

ON THE WATER, SEA OF GALILEE

4

¹One day as Jesus was standing by the Lake of Gennesaret, the people were crowding around him and listening to the word of God. ² He saw at the water's edge two boats, left there by the fishermen, who were washing their nets. ³ He got into one of the boats, the one belonging to Simon, and asked him to put out a little from shore. Then he sat down and taught the people from the boat.

⁴ When he had finished speaking, he said to Simon, "Put out into deep water, and let down the nets for a catch."

⁵ Simon answered, "Master, we've worked hard all night and haven't caught anything. But because you say so, I will let down the nets."

⁶ When they had done so, they caught such a large number of fish that their nets began to break.

⁷ So they signaled their partners in the other boat to come and help them, and they came and filled both boats so full that they began to sink.

⁸ When Simon Peter saw this, he fell at Jesus' knees and said, "Go away from me, Lord; I am a sinful man!" ⁹ For he and all his companions were astonished at the catch of fish they had taken, ¹⁰ and so were James and John, the sons of Zebedee, Simon's partners.

Then Jesus said to Simon, "Don't be afraid; from now on you will fish for people." ¹¹ So they pulled their boats up on shore, left everything and followed him.

Luke 5: 1-11 (NIV)

Simon Peter and his band of brothers had no idea that the shores of this water they'd grown up on, would soon become their seminary. And that although 100 miles from Jerusalem where all the religious elite sat near the holy of holies, that they—these common, ordinary fishermen—would be the ones to sit at the feet of the Rabbi of all rabbis, *and the holiest of them all.*

There will be many more life-changing moments on these familiar shores, but this moment with Jesus on the Sea of Galilee ushers in all the other moments that are to come. For Simon Peter, specifically, this moment Jesus calls him will change his life forever. This sacred moment is recorded in each of the three Synoptic Gospels—Matthew, Mark, and Luke. And while the Gospels all give a similar synopsis, they each provide different details along the way. Luke gives some specific details of this incredibly important day that Jesus officially calls His first disciples. This is another one of those interactions that would have been interesting to witness in person. From the context, we understand that these fishermen have worked all night with only empty nets to show for it. Then, Jesus gets into one of the boats and begins to use it as His podium of sorts, teaching to the crowds that had gathered, with His voice echoing across the water.

> When he had finished speaking, he said to Simon, "Put out into deep water, and let down the nets for a catch." Simon answered, "Master, we've worked hard all night and haven't caught anything. But because you say so, I will let down the nets."

Don't you wish we could hear the tone of Peter's voice as he responds to Jesus? One can only assume that after having worked all night, he's not only physically exhausted but maybe feeling defeated as well. And then someone who is *not* a fisherman starts advising the career fishermen, on how they should do their job. Is there sarcasm in Peter's voice? Is he frustrated by the suggestion of this outsider? No matter his posture, or the sound of his voice or look on his face, he decides to lower the nets into the water they'd already been fishing in all night. Nothing could have prepared these fishermen for the wonder they are about to experience.

> When they had done so, they caught such a large number of fish that their nets began to break. So they signaled their partners in the other boat to come and help them, and they came and filled both boats so full that they began to sink.

Only moments before, these fishermen were ending an unsuccessful night of work with empty nets. And then, in a moment, *Jesus changes everything.* The nets, once empty, and now bursting with fish, are only the beginning of the miracles on the shore that day.

There is something so deeply personal and sacred about the way of God towards His people. No one knows His creation better than the Creator Himself. He speaks into the deepest parts of our souls, using the words of our own "heart language." When Missionaries seek the most effective way to communicate the gospel of Jesus Christ, they often translate it into the heart language of those who are hearing the good news. Linguistically, it's common for a country to have a national language. But often within that, there is an even more specific communal language that is the most natural and comfortable. This heart language is what the everyday people use to communicate with each other as they live, and work, and play, and love.

As we look back through Scripture, we can see the incredibly intentional way that God reaches down into the lives of His people, speaking their heart language. To speak to the heart of the Magi, He spoke the language of the stars. To capture the heart of the shepherd, He spoke of sheep and flocks. To draw in the hearts of every day, working people, He used word pictures about water and bread, seeds and fruit, light and darkness. And we see here in this passage, that to communicate to the hearts of these fishermen…to give them true understanding, and to speak a language that they know better than they know themselves…He uses the language of *fish.*[1]

Jesus meets them right where they are. He comes close, moving from the shore to the boat, and He speaks a language their hearts can understand. And for the first time, Simon Peter and the other fishermen begin to see with their own eyes, the holiness that breaks into the familiar world they'd always known. From waters that had been scarce with fish and nets that had been glaringly empty, Jesus performs a miracle that day. In a moment, their nets become so full of fish, that they begin to break. And while filling the nets supernaturally with fish is a sign and wonder that catches their attention, it is perhaps, just a way that *Jesus speaks the heart language of these fishermen, paving the way for even bigger miracles to come.*

FISHING NET, SEA OF GALILEE

5

¹⁻³Once when he was standing on the shore of Lake Gennesaret, the crowd was pushing in on him to better hear the Word of God. He noticed two boats tied up. The fishermen had just left them and were out scrubbing their nets. He climbed into the boat that was Simon's and asked him to put out a little from the shore. Sitting there, using the boat for a pulpit, he taught the crowd.

⁴When he finished teaching, he said to Simon, "Push out into deep water and let your nets out for a catch."

⁵⁻⁷Simon said, "Master, we've been fishing hard all night and haven't caught even a minnow. But if you say so, I'll let out the nets." It was no sooner said than done—a huge haul of fish, straining the nets past capacity. They waved to their partners in the other boat to come help them. They filled both boats, nearly swamping them with the catch.

¹⁰⁻¹¹Simon Peter, when he saw it, fell to his knees before Jesus. "Master, leave. I'm a sinner and can't handle this holiness. Leave me to myself." When they pulled in that catch of fish, awe overwhelmed Simon and everyone with him. It was the same with James and John, Zebedee's sons, coworkers with Simon.

¹⁰⁻¹¹ Jesus said to Simon, "There is nothing to fear. From now on you'll be fishing for men and women." They pulled their boats up on the beach, left them, nets and all, and followed him.

Luke 5:1-11 (MSG)

Imagine for a moment, what it would look like to have your very best day—a day that would go down as your personal best in terms of your work, or school, or home life. Imagine a day where everything somehow aligns, and you are more productive than you'd ever thought possible, more successful than you ever dreamed, and the work of your hands and your heart far exceed your own expectations. This is that kind of day for Peter. Yet in spite of all that he witnesses, he gives it all up in a moment, just to be with Jesus.

It would be understandable to stop and think about how much money such an incredible catch could bring in. We'd understand if there are cheers, as the fishermen begin to realize what an incredible catch might mean for their business, their families, and their reputations. And some of the fishermen that day might have had those thoughts as they hauled in the nets.

What we see in Peter though, is this incredible, humbling, life-changing epiphany. Peter is brought to his knees in humility, not because this incredible gift has landed in his lap, but because his eyes are opened to the Giver that is standing in front of him with an open hand.

In this passage, we get the privilege of watching the journey that Peter takes as he begins the day as a frustrated fisherman and ends the day as a convinced follower of Jesus. Peter chooses to walk away from everything in exchange for Christ Himself.

There, with boats almost sinking from the weight of the unbelievable catch, Jesus performs a second miracle that day. Breathing in the sea air, surrounded by a bounty of fish, there in the middle of a place he knows better than himself, Simon Peter's eyes are opened.

For the first time, Simon Peter begins to see who Jesus really is, and even more so, who he really is himself, in the presence of Christ. Right alongside the miracle of the fish is the even greater, more life-changing miracle of what happens inside Simon Peter.

The God he'd heard about his whole life, is standing before him, as a physical person clothed in majesty and power. And taking in the incredible weight of his holiness, Simon Peter falls to his knees in humility, so keenly aware of his own brokenness in light of the overwhelming fullness of God.

"I'm a sinner and can't handle this holiness."

Can there be a more honest confession? Realizing the weight of our own unworthiness, in light of Christ's complete worthiness, is truly a miracle, isn't it? Each time one of us comes to see who we really are in light of Christ is a life-changing moment. To see who Jesus is and who we are *in* Him ushers in a necessary brokenness that helps us to see everything more clearly.

It's not just that we see our own sinful nature, but that we recognize our own inability to make a way to a perfect and Holy God. Still, we see His hand reaching out toward ours, bridging the gap, and stepping *toward* us in all our inadequacies. The miracle happens when we see rightly who God is, who we are, and how He is inviting us to Himself, and in fact, *making the way*.

Simon Peter is afraid of his own humbling realization and brought to his knees by the distance between himself and Jesus. But the miracle isn't over yet. Peter's realization of who Jesus really is—his understanding of the distance between his own sin and the holiness of Jesus—is the beginning step on his soul's journey to feeling its worth. Feeling the weight of his own brokenness and sin, Peter says,

"go away from me, Lord; I am a sinful man!"

But Peter, still on his knees in humility, raises his head up to see that *Jesus isn't going away at all.* He is, in fact, *continuing to stand right there, extending the invitation, even still.*

It's a miracle that can only be seen from a posture of humility and brokenness. We see the miracle ourselves when we realize who Jesus is, who we are *in* Him, and we allow it to change everything. When we realize that our best day, filled with all the success we can imagine, still pales in comparison to being near Jesus, Himself.

Unless we understand the difference, we are just fishermen, satisfied by the greatest catch. Unless our eyes are opened to the deeper invitation, we settle for one day's gift, instead of a life with the Giver of all good gifts.

That kind of miracle changes a life. It's the kind that makes you leave everything you've ever known and follow Him. Because once you've been close enough to truly see Jesus, being *with Him* is all that matters.

PETER'S HOUSE, CAPERNAUM

6

³⁰Now Simon's mother-in-law was lying sick with a fever; and immediately they spoke to Jesus about her.

³¹And He came to her and raised her up, taking her by the hand, and the fever left her, and she waited on them.

Mark 1:30, 31 (NASB)

Peter and the other disciples have been following Jesus as He preaches the good news and travels from town to town. They have been close enough to see with their own eyes as Jesus heals person after person, and ministers to those in the crowds. But what must it have been like for Peter to have that life-giving, healing touch of Jesus perform a miracle right in his own home? His wife's mother is dangerously sick with a high fever. Peter had seen Jesus bring miraculous healing countless times, but this time, someone he loved would be on the receiving end. Standing in his own home, watching someone in his own family creep dangerously towards death, Peter finds himself right in the wake of the miraculous.

Peter had seen Jesus heal the sick and he'd seen His holiness silence spirits, but those encounters had been with strangers in a crowd. On this day, the closeness of Jesus means that Peter is witnessing His miraculous power up close, in his own home, as he watches Jesus breathe life back into someone he loves. If Peter had been filled with awe and wonder, and maybe even admiration as he watched Jesus minister to strangers in a crowd, how much greater was his depth of reverence and gratitude when it was his own wife's mother whose life Jesus restored? Luke's account of this interaction says this—

> [38]Now Simon's mother-in-law was suffering from a high fever, and they asked Jesus to help her. [39]So he bent over her and rebuked the fever, and it left her. She got up at once and began to wait on them. (Luke 4:38-39 NIV)

Biblical historians suggest that during this season of Jesus' ministry, He would teach and preach, and serve the people in this area from His home base at Simon Peter's house, right near the synagogue in Capernaum.[1] How often had Jesus laid His head there to rest? How many meals had He eaten with Simon Peter's family around their table? Did He laugh with their children? Did He help with the dishes? Did He tell stories at night by the light of the fire?

We have no way of knowing just what those early days together looked like, but we do know that when one of his own is in need, Simon Peter asks Jesus to help. It's a revealing display of the way their friendship had become more personal and intimate as Jesus spent time in Simon Peter's home. And the fact that Simon Peter feels the freedom to ask for help on behalf of someone he loves is so telling. The Scripture says,

> "...and they asked Jesus to help her. So He bent over her and rebuked the fever, and it left her."

The original Greek word for "rebuked" here is *epitimaó*, which means "to forbid, to restrain, or to admonish."[2] This type of rebuke is "to warn by instructing," but its fundamental sense is "warning to prevent something from going wrong."[3] This word for the rebuke from Jesus is actually the same word used when Jesus, with God-given authority, commands the wind and the waves to obey Him and evil spirits to flee. It is miraculous in nature, and literally changes the course of what could happen it a moment.

God's power is on display by the complete authority of Jesus. The wind and the waves obey Him. Unclean spirits are forced to flee by the sound of His voice. Broken bodies are made whole with a touch of His hand. Jesus stands with the entire authority of Heaven in Him. The Gospel writer Matthew will later go on to write these words spoken by Jesus—"...all authority has been given to Me in heaven and earth." And right after this display of the complete authority of Jesus, Matthew records this promise that quickly comes after—"*and I am with you always.*"

The person of Jesus Christ holds complete authority. And the very nature of Jesus is that He is, *Immanuel, God with us.* He is the very nature of God yet in the form of a man. In Him, we find complete authority, but also nearness. He is mighty in power, but also, as close as our breath. The authority of Heaven is brought to earth in the person of Jesus.

He is with us. So perhaps, more amazing than the sheer power of Jesus to command the wind, the waves, and a rising fever, is *the closeness of Jesus even to see it at all.*

He is not a God that sits high in the clouds over His world, far below. He is with us *at* the table. He is *beside* us on the path. He is *above* the very ones we love, bending down close to see. He is close enough *to be with us*—to speak into our very lives as they are happening.

Maybe what's most miraculous about Jesus in this interaction at Simon Peter's house is not the power held in the actions of Jesus—in the rebuking and the healing—but in the position of being *with*. He is near. He is close.

Some translations of Psalm 18:35 display how David speaks back to the heart of God about His nearness saying, "*You stoop down to make me great.*"[4]

In this encounter, Jesus is the very picture of that heart of God toward us. He stoops down, takes our hand, and raises us up.

Jesus is with us. Not just *for* us, not just *above* us, not just *over* us, but *with us*. Bending down close to see, and in gentleness speaking in—breathing life and grace and healing, right where we are today.

SYNAGOGUE AT CAPERNAUM

7

[28] Immediately the news about Him spread everywhere into all the surrounding district of Galilee. [29] And immediately after they came out of the synagogue, they came into the house of Simon and Andrew, with James and John.

[30] Now Simon's mother-in-law was lying sick with a fever; and immediately they spoke to Jesus about her. [31] And He came to her and raised her up, taking her by the hand, and the fever left her, and she waited on them. [32] When evening came, after the sun had set, they began bringing to Him all who were ill and those who were demon-possessed. [33] And the whole city had gathered at the door. [34] And He healed many who were ill with various diseases, and cast out many demons; and He was not permitting the demons to speak, because they knew who He was.

[35] In the early morning, while it was still dark, Jesus got up, left the house, and went away to a secluded place, and was praying there. [36] Simon and his companions searched for Him; [37] they found Him, and said to Him, "Everyone is looking for You." [38] He said to them, "Let us go somewhere else to the towns nearby, so that I may preach there also; for that is what I came for."

Mark 1:28-38 (NASB)

In a private moment, Jesus had healed Peter's Mother-in-law. He'd breathed life back into her, and soon, she was up and serving her family again, almost as if nothing had happened. He'd already healed the sick as crowds had gathered and seen His miraculous power. But healing Peter's mother-in-law hadn't been for the masses. It had been behind closed doors with people He'd come to love. It wasn't a public display of His power, but rather a tender, intimate display of His compassion and love.

Before this private moment, the news of Jesus was already beginning to travel into all the surrounding areas of Galilee. Word of this extraordinary man that preached good news and healed the sick spread throughout the land like wildfire. Careful not to break the law and "work" on the sacred Sabbath, desperate people from all the surrounding areas wait until dusk and as the stars begin to take their place in the sky, the Sabbath day ends, and the people start to line up to see Jesus.

Gathering outside Peter's house, people from everywhere, with all sorts of needs wait their turn to see Jesus. "*The whole city had gathered at the door.*" The people in the crowds that day, outside of Peter's home want more than a glimpse of Jesus. They want a miracle. They want healing.

Of course, we can't know if the people in this particular crowd truly understand who Jesus is and the gospel that He'd come to preach. We know that many that surrounded Jesus in the early days of His public ministry did so not because they wanted to follow His gospel and be changed by His teaching, but because they *wanted* something from Him. They were attracted to His supernatural power and what He could do to meet their needs. And Jesus healed them. He cast out demons. He changed the lives of the people in the crowd that day forever. And after spending hours with those lined up outside Peter's house, we see Jesus doing the most remarkable thing.

> **In the early morning, while it was still dark, Jesus got up, left the house, and went away to a secluded place, and was praying there.**

Even Jesus needs time alone with the Father. Even Jesus needs rest. He lives in the rhythm of serving, pouring out, and loving those around Him well. Jesus prioritizes time alone with the Father even in—*perhaps especially in*—times of high demand. This is one of many times we see Jesus retreating to a quiet place alone during a busy season of His ministry. It is a value to Jesus to intentionally turn His eyes back to the Father in these moments. Especially when He is pouring out, Jesus turns to the Father to fill up His own cup again.

And the fascinating thing is, not everybody understands—*not even Peter*. All Peter knows is that there are still more people looking for Jesus. They search for Him, and when they find Him, Peter says, "*everyone is looking for you.*" Even in Peter's mind, there is an expectation of Jesus. It isn't the first time Jesus will be misunderstood and isn't the last time He models what it looks like to rest, and to be alone with the Father, even when demands press in at every side.

Jesus comes away from His time alone with the Father refreshed and with a clarity of mission. His time of rest and prayer only deepens His resolve to keep going and to keep preaching the good news. There are people in the towns nearby that need to hear the message of the gospel. His mission is clear, and while He loves and serves those that come to Him, His eyes always remain fixed on the Father, and the reason He'd come.

His time of rest, alone with the Father, renews the clarity of His mission and the passion in His soul.

Time alone with God does that for us, doesn't it? Even when things press in on every side—even when everywhere we look there are needs—time alone with the Father gives us clarity on how to best spend our days for the glory of God and the good of others.

Even as needs arise all around Him, Jesus is so in tune with the Father, that He is able to discern when it is time to serve and pour out and when it is time to stop and be filled up. He'd said in John 5:19—

> "…the Son can do nothing of his own accord, but only what he sees the Father doing. For whatever the Father does, that the Son does likewise."

It's in the quiet that everything else falls away, and we can hear the Father's voice again. *And His voice brings clarity and peace for our next steps. It's in the secret place alone with God that our souls find their rest.* It's something Jesus teaches Peter that day, and something He is still teaching us today too.

THE GALILEE

8

⁴⁰ Now when Jesus returned, a crowd welcomed him, for they were all expecting him. ⁴¹ Then a man named Jairus, a synagogue leader, came and fell at Jesus' feet, pleading with him to come to his house ⁴² because his only daughter, a girl of about twelve, was dying.

As Jesus was on his way, the crowds almost crushed him. ⁴³ And a woman was there who had been subject to bleeding for twelve years, but no one could heal her. ⁴⁴ She came up behind him and touched the edge of his cloak, and immediately her bleeding stopped.

⁴⁵ "Who touched me?" Jesus asked. When they all denied it, Peter said, "Master, the people are crowding and pressing against you."

⁴⁶ But Jesus said, "Someone touched me; I know that power has gone out from me." ⁴⁷ Then the woman, seeing that she could not go unnoticed, came trembling and fell at his feet. In the presence of all the people, she told why she had touched him and how she had been instantly healed. ⁴⁸ Then he said to her, "Daughter, your faith has healed you. Go in peace."

⁴⁹ While Jesus was still speaking, someone came from the house of Jairus, the synagogue leader. "Your daughter is dead," he said. "Don't bother the teacher anymore."

⁵⁰ Hearing this, Jesus said to Jairus, "Don't be afraid; just believe, and she will be healed." ⁵¹ When he arrived at the house of Jairus, he did not let anyone go in with him except Peter, John and James, and the child's father and mother. ⁵² Meanwhile, all the people were wailing and mourning for her. "Stop wailing," Jesus said. "She is not dead but asleep."

⁵³ They laughed at him, knowing that she was dead. ⁵⁴ But he took her by the hand and said, "My child, get up!" ⁵⁵ Her spirit returned, and at once she stood up. Then Jesus told them to give her something to eat. ⁵⁶ Her parents were astonished, but he ordered them not to tell anyone what had happened.

Luke 8:40-56 (NIV)

In the last few passages, we have taken note of the closeness of Jesus. Today we see the closeness *of Peter to Jesus*, which allows him to bear witness to one of the most incredibly significant encounters of Jesus ever recorded. Peter is one of the few people to witness both of these encounters within this passage. This beloved story in Scripture teaches Peter, and us right along with him, so much about the heart of Jesus.

The passage opens in a large crowd with several people present and ends behind closed doors, where Peter is one of only a few select people that Jesus invites into a secret and sacred moment. This encounter displays an accurate picture of the juxtaposition of two very different people with two very different backgrounds, lives, and circumstances. Yet somehow, both find themselves desperate and very much in need of the healing touch of Jesus.

Jairus is a respected man of position, very likely wealthy, whose only daughter is so sick that she is on the brink of death. The woman with the issue of blood has spent all the money she had, but no doctor has been able to heal her. Seen as "unclean," she's been forced to live alone as an outcast. The juxtaposition of these two very different people approaching Jesus reveals the very different places from which they each come. Jairus is the head of the synagogue. The woman, however, who is "ceremonially unclean," wouldn't have even been allowed inside the synagogue walls. Jairus has a family and a twelve-year-old daughter who is sick. The woman is all alone and has been sick for 12 years. Jairus has a position and a name everyone knows. The woman in this encounter is not even given a name here.

He is respected. She is rejected. And yet, they both reach such a point of desperation that their only hope is to reach out to Jesus. Suffering is no respecter of age, privilege or position, and here, we see that to be true. Two people, living completely different lives, both find themselves right in the middle of the pain and suffering of this broken world. But we also see there is no one too unclean or too insignificant to get Jesus' attention. And in the same way, there is no one so powerful or so privileged that they do not find themselves, at some point, in desperate need of Jesus.

Jairus, this respected synagogue leader, is so desperate because his only daughter is dying, that he falls at the feet of Jesus. Right there in front of the crowd, he makes his plea. The passage says,

"as Jesus was on His way, the crowds almost crushed Him."

The woman, carrying the same weight of desperation, thinks if only she could get close to Jesus, she could be healed. She comes up behind Him and *merely grabs ahold of the edge of His robe*. And in an instant, she is healed. And what happens next, is a moment we see so often with Jesus. He asks a question. He asks, not because He doesn't know, and needs help getting the answer. He asks to give the woman a chance to come forward.

Peter, of course, misses the cue that this question is not a literal request for information, but rather a personal invitation from Jesus.

> **Then the woman, seeing that she could not go unnoticed, came trembling and fell at his feet. In the presence of all the people, she told why she had touched him and how she had been instantly healed. Then he said to her, "Daughter, your faith has healed you. Go in peace."**

She comes to Jesus in a hidden moment, within the chaos of the crowd, and yet in His compassion, He brings her into the light. He sees her, He heals her, and He brings peace to her pain. Jesus stops everything for this woman—a woman who, for so long, had been isolated and rejected. He gives her His full attention and a chance to be seen and heard. He positions her "*in the presence of all the people*" to give testimony to her incredibly powerful faith and in doing so, an invitation to not just physical healing, but true restoration in Jesus. And then, right there in front of the same crowd, Jesus gives this woman a sacred gift.

This woman had been made to live alone as an outcast. She is no one's daughter and has no one pleading on her behalf. Jesus is already on His way to help Jairus, and yet, He takes a moment to stop and breathe life back into this woman, too. He elevates her, applauds her great faith, and with incredible tenderness and compassion, calls her "*Daughter.*" In an instant, full healing replaces her desperation. The original Greek words used in this passage describe her physical healing, but also how her faith in Jesus restores her, saves her, and brings ultimate healing to both her body and soul. She finds restoration and true healing in Jesus, as He says to her, "*Daughter, your faith has healed you. Go in peace.*"

It must have been a sacred moment to watch. And yet, it seems that while Jesus stops to interact with the woman, it means that time has run out for Jairus and his daughter. In the moments that Jesus has stopped to heal the woman, Jairus receives word that his daughter has died. But Jesus turns His attention back to Jairus again saying, "Don't be afraid; just believe, and she will be healed."

When they get to the home of Jairus, Jesus only allows Peter, James, and John to join the girls' parents inside. Now behind closed doors in a quiet, sacred, and even secret moment, Jesus answers the prayers of Jairus, too. Jesus takes her hand, and with His words, *He literally breathes life back into the little girl.*

In that room, Peter witnesses another life-changing miracle of Jesus. Sometimes Jesus gives us a glimpse into the miraculous ways He is moving, and working, and bringing life. Sometimes that happens "in the presence of the people," and just as it was for Peter in this interaction, sometimes Jesus invites us into the secret and the sacred with just Him.

One of the incredible things Peter witnesses that day first hand is the way that Jesus responds to what we would often see as "interruptions." In reading the Gospels, we see over and over again, that often something we might perceive as an inconvenience, Jesus merely views as an opportunity—a chance to show someone they are seen, heard, and loved. It is challenging, convicting, and inspiring to see the way Jesus freely responds in these life-changing encounters with the countless people that God brings into His path. In His willingness to be interrupted, He prioritizes those people, and the sacred encounters He has with them, over the importance of sticking to the perceived agenda, at the time. We would do well to pray for eyes to be opened to see things the way Jesus does—to learn what it looks like to respond to interruptions with the same grace and openness.

C.S. Lewis once wrote, "the great thing, if one can, is to stop regarding all the unpleasant things as interruptions of one's 'own' or 'real' life. The truth is of course that what one calls the interruptions are precisely real life—the life God is sending one day by day."[1]

As we'll see later on this journey, one day, Jesus will charge Peter with the job of shepherding His flock and feeding and caring for His people, as Jesus builds His Church. His interactions with Jairus and the woman give Peter a beautiful display of the way Jesus interacts with both the esteemed, respected people as well as the poor and the rejected. It makes sense that Jesus gives Peter a front row seat to the upside-down ways of the Kingdom, and what it can look like to care for people…*all people*, in the Kingdom of God.

Rich or poor, esteemed or rejected, powerful or powerless, well-known or unseen—each one of us is in need of the healing that can only be found by Jesus. And in His great mercy, He extends His healing hand of hope and grace to all of us.

NIGHT ON THE SEA OF GALILEE

9

²² Immediately Jesus made the disciples get into the boat and go on ahead of him to the other side, while he dismissed the crowd. ²³ After he had dismissed them, he went up on a mountainside by himself to pray. Later that night, he was there alone, ²⁴ and the boat was already a considerable distance from land, buffeted by the waves because the wind was against it.

²⁵ Shortly before dawn Jesus went out to them, walking on the lake. ²⁶ When the disciples saw him walking on the lake, they were terrified. "It's a ghost," they said, and cried out in fear.

²⁷ But Jesus immediately said to them: "Take courage! It is I. Don't be afraid."

²⁸ "Lord, if it's you," Peter replied, "tell me to come to you on the water."

²⁹ "Come," he said.

Then Peter got down out of the boat, walked on the water and came toward Jesus.

Matthew 14:22-29 (NIV)

If you grew up in church, you may have learned about this story in Sunday School. If this story is familiar, try reading it today with fresh eyes, as though you've never heard it before. The events unfold almost as if they are scenes written for a movie. Can you imagine witnessing this? There is so much to take in here, and if we look closely, there are some incredible things we can learn from both Jesus and Peter.

In this iconic interaction, the disciples have been following Jesus for a year or possibly, two. In Matthew 14, the disciples and Jesus have just learned the overwhelming and heartbreaking news about the tragic beheading of John the Baptist. As you can imagine, this hits close to home, not only for the disciples but for Jesus as well. In the text right before our passage today, we see Jesus, undoubtedly grieving, trying to retreat by Himself in a boat on the Sea of Galilee. The crowds, however, determined to see Him just went to the other side and waited for Him there.

Yet again we see Jesus view the multitudes following Him not as an inconvenience or interruption. Instead, the text says, "when He went ashore, He saw great multitudes, and He felt compassion for them." Despite His own desire to rest, and be alone with the Father, Jesus spoke to the people who came to see Him and healed many while He was there.

When the disciples get to Him, they want to send the crowds away, but Jesus knows the people are tired and hungry. And in His great compassion, He gives them a meal they will never forget. Jesus takes five loaves of bread and two fish and turns it into more than enough. In the hands of Jesus, the meal becomes a miracle and feeds more than *five thousand people* that day.

In light of everything that happens, the crowds gravitate to the power they see in Jesus. John chapter 6 tells us that Jesus perceives that they literally want to make Him king, right there at that moment, by force! Jesus sends the disciples away because He knows that at this point, they all really still see Him in terms of earthly power. They don't yet understand fully, who He is.

So this is where we pick up in Matthew 14, on this surreal night during a storm. The sea's location makes it subject to sudden and violent storms as the wind comes over the eastern mountains and drops suddenly onto the sea.[1]

There are two times in Scripture, where we see the disciples getting into some trouble in the waters. Earlier in the Gospels, we read the story of the time that Jesus and the disciples are in the boat together when a storm comes and Jesus is sleeping. In that story, Jesus is *in* the boat with them, and when they wake Him, He commands the wind and waves to calm down, and they obey Him!

The story we read today is the second time they run into trouble on the water, but this time is a bit different. Jesus is not with the disciples in the boat, but, as Mark's account tells us, He is watching and is close enough to see them.

> [47]When it was evening, the boat was in the middle of the sea, and He was alone on the land. [48]Seeing them straining at the oars, for the wind was against them, at about the fourth watch of the night He came to them, walking on the sea; and He intended to pass by them. [49]But when they saw Him walking on the sea, they supposed that it was a ghost, and cried out; [50]for they all saw Him and were terrified. But immediately He spoke with them and said to them, "Take courage; it is I, do not be afraid." (Mark 6:47-50 NASB)

Jesus is alone on the mountain, and even though it is the middle of the night and He has retreated to pray, He sees that His disciples are in distress on the water. The Greek word used here describes how the disciples are literally "tormented" as they are struggling in the wind and the waves.[2] The last time they had been in such distress on the water, Jesus called out and calmed the wind and the waves. This time, Jesus is close enough to see them struggling, and in their time of need goes to them.

He enters the storm to be with them, even though He has been with them all along. The disciples are exhausted and terrified, and then they see this thing moving toward them, walking on water. They can't even make sense of it, and in their fear, they think it is a ghost. Seeing them in their fear and distress, Jesus speaks peace. "*Take courage, it is I, do not be afraid.*"

We learn so much about Jesus here. And also, Peter. And even still, ourselves. This passage reminds us that Jesus is present with us in our storms, too. We aren't ever promised a life without storms. But Jesus does promise that in the storm, He is there with us. He's actually been there all along. *He sees us.* He is close. He knows what is happening in our lives. He is right there with us in it all.

Jesus meets our struggle and our fear with His peace. Sometimes He brings His peace by calming the wind and the waves around us. And sometimes, He sees our struggle and fear and walks right into the storm to be with us.

The way Peter responds in the middle of this storm is both profound and noteworthy, as well. When Peter sees Jesus walking towards them in the storm, he cries out, "Lord, if it's you, tell me to come to you on the water." *Peter wants to be near Jesus.* And Peter models for us, the choice we all have in how we respond when we too, find ourselves in the middle of a storm.

It would be easy to assume that this iconic story and moment between Jesus and His disciples and Peter is *just for them.* But the truth is, this passage isn't just about what happened that night in the middle of the storm. *This passage reminds us all over again, of the true character of God.* Jesus coming to be with them in the storm is not just something that happened one time on the boat with Peter and the disciples. It is a story of God, and His people, and His promise for all of us. The relationship between Jesus and Peter is, so often, a picture of God's relationship with us. And it is a picture of His promise to be with us always.

This has always been the heart of God for His people. It's a promise that has echoed throughout the generations. Long ago to the people of Israel, that night on the water with Peter and the disciples, and even still to each of us today, this is His promise to us—

> [1]"Do not fear, for I have redeemed you; I have summoned you by name; you are mine. [2]When you pass through the waters, I will be with you; and when you pass through the rivers, they will not sweep over you. When you walk through the fire, you will not be burned; the flames will not set you ablaze. [3]For I am the Lord your God, the Holy One of Israel, your Savior." (Isaiah 43: 1-3 NIV)

OUT OF THE BOAT, THE SEA OF GALILEE

10

[27]But Jesus immediately said to them: "Take courage! It is I. Don't be afraid."

[28]"Lord, if it's you," Peter replied, "tell me to come to you on the water."

[29]"Come," he said.

Then Peter got down out of the boat, walked on the water and came toward Jesus. [30]But when he saw the wind, he was afraid and, beginning to sink, cried out, "Lord, save me!"

[31]Immediately Jesus reached out his hand and caught him. "You of little faith," he said, "why did you doubt?"

[32]And when they climbed into the boat, the wind died down. [33]Then those who were in the boat worshiped him, saying, "Truly you are the Son of God."

Matthew 14: 27-33 (NIV)

Have you ever wondered what you would do, if you had been on that boat in the middle of the storm, in the middle of the lake, in the middle of the night? It says the disciples are afraid, and they cry out in fear. That sounds about right. Everything about this scene is frightening. But immediately Jesus said to them, "take courage! It is I. Don't be afraid." We can learn a lot about Jesus by how He sees the disciples and enters the storm to be with them, bringing them peace. We also learn a lot about Peter by what happens next.

Long before this night on the water, we learn that Peter is bold and passionate. He so often jumps in with his whole heart, usually without stopping to think first. He acts on impulse and fully follows his heart. He doesn't wait to see proof. We see that work both to his favor and to his detriment. Even though we see Peter as a bold, lion-hearted, quick-moving follower, there is also something deeply discerning in his spirit that we begin to see uncovered in this passage.

It must feel like a dream. The wind is whipping, tossing the boat. The darkness of the night covers them. Jesus, sensing their fear and confusion, speaks right to them. And like when a baby hears its mother or father and immediately calms, the sound of Jesus' voice begins to bring peace, diffusing the fear that hangs in the air.

"Take courage, it is I; do not be afraid."

Peter's first instinct here gives us such a clear picture of his heart and the type of man he is. Instead of shrinking back in fear, or even pausing to attempt to understand the situation unfolding before him, Peter just simply wants *to be near Jesus.* Even though it must feel unsettling to be tossed around on the boat in the midst of a storm, most of us would assume that surely being *in* the boat is a better alternative to being *out* of the boat?

Not for Peter. *He wants to be with Jesus.* And there is something so meaningful about the way this scene unfolds.

**"Lord, if it's you," Peter replied, "tell me to come to you on the water." "Come,"
he said. Then Peter got down out of the boat, walked on the water and came
toward Jesus.**

Despite his own fear and confusion, Peter decides that being near Jesus is the safest place to be. And although the other disciples surround him, *Peter is the only one in the boat to have this response.* There is an unmistakable humility in the way that Peter is drawn to Jesus, and even more so, in the way, he says, "Lord, if it's you, tell me to come to you on the water."

Peter instinctively understands that it must be Jesus that calls him out. He recognizes that the power of stepping out on to the water has to be in response to the invitation of Jesus. "Come," Jesus says, calling him out where no one has ever stepped before. And defying every signal his body must have been sending him, Peter willingly decides to leave the shelter of the boat and to step out into the rough waters. Peter doesn't analyze or wait for proof. He believes the words of Jesus and he trusts in His power, more than even gravity, in this moment. His faith in Jesus is greater than anything he'd ever seen with his own eyes, so when Jesus calls to him, Peter responds.

Peter steps out of the boat, onto the water. What courage! What faith! What belief in the One who has called him out onto the waves. Peter responds to the call of Jesus, and in doing so, steps right into a miracle.

The impossible becomes possible because Jesus makes it so. With eyes fixed on Jesus, Peter walks on water. But in a moment, Peter's eyes shift from Jesus to the wind and the waves, and in an instant, Peter begins to sink. Peter had no doubt when he first jumped onto the water, but right there in the middle of the miraculous, Peter takes his eyes of Jesus. He sees the wind and the waves, and begins to sink! Without proof, he had just walked on water! But when his gaze shifts away from Jesus, his faith begins to falter. And suddenly, he needs proof that the impossible thing happening is actually possible!

Maybe Peter needs to sink to experience what it feels like to be saved. Maybe he needs to feel the nearness of Jesus, and to trust in His power, and to see His power show itself to be steady and sure, even in the moments when his own faith wavers.

Though Peter is the only one to step out onto the water, there is a lesson here for all of us. When Jesus calls us out onto the water, with our eyes on Him, the miraculous becomes possible.

He is right there with us, in our most significant moments of surrender. And He is also there, with the covering of His perfect Covenant love, even when our commitment falters and our faith trembles. He is with us in the storm, reaching out His hand to catch us in the moments when we begin to slip beneath the crashing waves. Should our eyes look to the left and the right, we might find ourselves sinking in fear and disbelief. But Jesus is there in that moment too, reaching out His hand to save.

Those are the moments that, like Peter, we see that our own faith and commitment pale in comparison to the sureness of His steady hand and the wonder of His miraculous Covenant love for us. Those are the moments that build our faith. Those moments of complete surrender uncover what our eyes are truly fixed upon, and reveal places in us that have been built on shifting sand. When we step out of the boat, we see and feel, just like water under our feet, the miraculous, wondrous nearness of Jesus Himself. Scripture describes how this surreal night on the water ends.

> **And when they climbed into the boat, the wind died down. Then those who were in the boat worshiped him, saying, "Truly you are the Son of God."**

And just like that, in the middle of the storm, in the middle of the lake, in the middle of the night, Jesus brings His peace. Jesus calls Peter out onto the water that night, but He also gives Peter an invitation, further up and further in, to a life of surrender. Peter is the only one to step out of the boat and walk on the water to Jesus on this night. But each of them there in the boat become witnesses to a miracle they'll not soon forget.

So today, whether you find yourself safe inside the boat, or in the middle of your own walk of surrender upon the crashing waves, *Jesus remains the same.* He is close, with His hand reaching out, to bring His peace right in the middle of the storm. And just as it is for the disciples, may we find ourselves there today, with eyes fixed on Jesus, responding to His invitation to surrender with a heart of worship.

BOAT ON THE SEA OF GALILEE

11

²³ Then some boats from Tiberias landed near the place where the people had eaten the bread after the Lord had given thanks. ²⁴ Once the crowd realized that neither Jesus nor his disciples were there, they got into the boats and went to Capernaum in search of Jesus. ²⁵ When they found him on the other side of the lake, they asked him, "Rabbi, when did you get here?" ²⁶ Jesus answered, "Very truly I tell you, you are looking for me, not because you saw the signs I performed but because you ate the loaves and had your fill. ²⁷ Do not work for food that spoils, but for food that endures to eternal life, which the Son of Man will give you. For on him God the Father has placed his seal of approval." ²⁸ Then they asked him, "What must we do to do the works God requires?" ²⁹ Jesus answered, "The work of God is this: to believe in the one he has sent." ³⁰ So they asked him, "What sign then will you give that we may see it and believe you? What will you do? ³¹ Our ancestors ate the manna in the wilderness; as it is written: 'He gave them bread from heaven to eat.'" ³² Jesus said to them, "Very truly I tell you, it is not Moses who has given you the bread from heaven, but it is my Father who gives you the true bread from heaven. ³³ For the bread of God is the bread that comes down from heaven and gives life to the world." ³⁴ "Sir," they said, "always give us this bread." ³⁵ Then Jesus declared, "I am the bread of life. Whoever comes to me will never go hungry, and whoever believes in me will never be thirsty." ⁴⁷ "Very truly I tell you, the one who believes has eternal life. ⁴⁸ I am the bread of life. ⁴⁹ Your ancestors ate the manna in the wilderness, yet they died. ⁵⁰ But here is the bread that comes down from heaven, which anyone may eat and not die. ⁵¹ I am the living bread that came down from heaven. Whoever eats this bread will live forever. This bread is my flesh, which I will give for the life of the world…" ⁵⁹ He said this while teaching in the synagogue in Capernaum. ⁶⁰ On hearing it, many of his disciples said, "This is a hard teaching. Who can accept it?" ⁶⁶ From this time many of his disciples turned back and no longer followed him. ⁶⁷ "You do not want to leave too, do you?" Jesus asked the Twelve. ⁶⁸ Simon Peter answered him, "Lord, to whom shall we go? You have the words of eternal life. ⁶⁹ We have come to believe and to know that you are the Holy One of God."

John 6:23-35, 47-51, 59-60, 66-69 (NIV)

Peter and the disciples are beginning to see that many will eventually come to know—the gospel of Jesus Christ may be simple, *but it is certainly not easy to comprehend.*

At the beginning of John, Chapter 6, a large crowd had gathered, and the disciples asked Jesus, "Where are we to buy bread, that these may eat?" Jesus went on to take a young boy's five loaves of bread and two fish and multiplied them. Miraculously, in the hands of Jesus, it became more than enough for everyone. John 6:14 says, "after the people saw the sign Jesus performed, they began to say, 'Surely this is the Prophet who is to come into the world.'"

Jesus had moved miraculously, and the signs and wonders witnessed that day had been intended to illuminate who Jesus truly is. But instead of their hearts being drawn to Jesus, many were drawn to the miracle itself. Mark 6:52 describes it this way—

> "…They had not gained any insight from the incident of the loaves,
> but their heart was hardened."

The words that Jesus speaks in our passage today become all the more poignant when we realize that He was speaking on a much deeper level—speaking into much more profound things than it may seem, at first. In verse 26, Jesus says,

> "Very truly I tell you, you are looking for me, not because you saw the signs I
> performed but because you ate the loaves and had your fill."

This is so much deeper than a conversation about bread. Jesus knows that the miracle of the loaves and fish is still fresh in their minds, both for the disciples and the crowds that had gathered. And He uses the picture of the loaves of bread and physical hunger to help give them eyes to see *the deeper longing inside and the only thing that will ever satisfy that hunger.* Some will begin to see that clearly. Others will not.

Jesus is the Bread of Life, and what He offers is the only thing that can satisfy the longing deep in our souls. Faith in Jesus will be the only thing to satisfy the hunger. When He speaks of eating His flesh—taking His body and blood—many cannot yet understand what His words mean. The people have a reference for the manna from the past, but they have no reference for a Savior that would give the gift of eternal life with the sacrifice of His body and blood. It is a picture of the New Covenant to come, and like a kaleidoscope of moving shapes and colors before them, they are beginning to see it, but they cannot yet comprehend it, in full. It says that when many of His disciples heard it, they said, "This teaching is difficult; who can accept it?"

They're right. *This teaching is difficult.* It's far too wondrous for our feeble minds to comprehend fully.

For some, when they hear the words of Jesus and a gospel that defies all logic, it is too much for them. Jesus had said, "The work of God is this: to believe in the one He has sent."

For some, the act of believing is simply too great a task. The call to have faith in what mere minds cannot comprehend eventually becomes a line in the sand. And verse 66 says, "From this time many of his disciples *turned back and no longer followed him.*" But when Jesus asked the Twelve if they too wanted to leave, *it is Peter, the Rock* that speaks collectively on their behalf.

> [68-69]Peter replied, "Master, to whom would we go? You have the words of real life,
> eternal life. We've already committed ourselves, confident that you are the Holy
> One of God." (John 6:68-69 MSG)

Peter and the others are beginning to see Jesus' deeper meaning, and they have begun the work of God—*to believe in the One He sent.* Bread satisfies the physical hunger within us, but hunger will always return. *Jesus is the Bread of Life, and whoever comes to Him will never go hungry, and whoever believes in Him will never be thirsty.*

Jesus is leaving the breadcrumb trail. Not everyone will follow, but Peter stays close and remains resolute in his commitment. It is interesting that Peter actually uses the words here, "we've already *committed* ourselves, confident that you are the Holy One of God."

Peter is unraveling the great mystery of the gospel. His eyes are opened, and he sees and believes that Jesus is the Holy One of God. But He doesn't see it fully yet. And while others who don't yet fully understand the mystery are beginning to fall away, Peter affirms his commitment. It's not yet time, but one day soon, Peter will hear Jesus again speak of Bread.

There will come a day when Peter will realize that *commitment to* Jesus is significant, but it is the *Covenant of Jesus that is greater still.* Like Peter, may each of us come to know that the offering of Jesus—*His Body, The Bread*—is what will fully satisfy the hunger and deepest longing of every heart.

GATES OF HELL, CAESEREA PHILIPPI

12

[13] When Jesus came to the region of Caesarea Philippi, he asked his disciples, "Who do people say that the Son of Man is?"

[14] They replied, "Some say John the Baptist; others, Elijah; still others, Jeremiah or one of the prophets."

[15] "But you," he asked them, "who do you say that I am?"
[16] Simon Peter answered, "You are the Messiah, the Son of the living God."

[17] Jesus responded, "Blessed are you, Simon son of Jonah, because flesh and blood did not reveal this to you, but my Father in heaven. [18] And I also say to you that you are Peter, and on this rock I will build my church, and the gates of Hades will not overpower it. [19] I will give you the keys of the kingdom of heaven, and whatever you bind on earth will have been bound in heaven, and whatever you loose on earth will have been loosed in heaven." [20] Then he gave the disciples orders to tell no one that he was the Messiah.

Matthew 16:13-20 (CSB)

At first glance, this seems like an odd interaction for Jesus to have with the disciples who have been following Him for a long time. Peter and the other disciples have been walking with Jesus, hearing Him teach, watching with their very own eyes as He heals the sick, makes the lame to walk, and casts out oppression from bodies and souls in great need of healing. But Jesus wants to give them an opportunity not just to observe, but to express in their own words, who He is.

The location of this interaction is noteworthy. Jesus takes the disciples to a place of deep symbolism as He begins this conversation. Caesarea Philippi was a pagan city that was filled with moral corruption and represented the worst evils of culture—a place known for idols, shrines, and immoral worship practices. Pagans believed that water symbolized the abyss and that caves were a door to the underworld. Because Caesarea Philippi stood near a cave with spring water flowing from it, the pagans thought of the cave as a gate to the underworld.[1] Because of this, the site was called "The Gates of Hell," and for the Jews, this setting was blasphemous and horrifying.[2] And yet *this* is where Jesus takes His disciples and where His exchange with them takes place as He asks the question....

> "Who do people say the Son of Man is?"

Their answers confirm that while they know a great deal, they certainly don't fully comprehend it all just yet.

> "But what about you?" he asked. "Who do you say I am?" Simon Peter answered,
> "You are the Messiah, the Son of the living God."

It would be easy for us to read right over Peter's response, because, *of course,* Jesus is the Messiah, the Son of the living God. But we have the advantage of already knowing the whole story.

Jesus had identified Himself as the Messiah before in answer to the observations of others, but not with plain and simple language. There had been a few times, that Jesus had spoken about who He was. Luke 4 gives us an account at the very beginning of His public ministry that Jesus revealed His true nature.

It hadn't been a flashy, public announcement, but for those present and paying attention, Jesus had declared that *He* had fulfilled Isaiah's foreshadowing of the One who was to come. And in the same way, John 4 records another interaction where Jesus confirms who He really is, not with a loud speech blatantly calling Himself God, but an affirmation that *He was* the One they knew was coming. For those seeking and listening closely, Jesus had affirmed He was Immanuel God with us, the Messiah, called the Christ. But He also spent those years just living right alongside them, walking among them, breathing in and out, just as fully human as they were.

So Jesus asks a fair question—"who do *you* say that I am." While Peter's answer seems appropriate to us, he really is answering a question that had probably not been directly asked or answered so plainly before. That makes his answer truly compelling. Peter and the other disciples are, of course, living this story in real time. They are learning day by day, more of who this incredibly mysterious and miraculous man really is and how He looks nothing like they'd expected but is everything their souls needed.

He teaches, and heals, and lives without sin. But at the same time, His stomach probably growls when He is hungry, and He falls asleep when He is tired, just like the people He is living alongside.

He is fully God and yet somehow, also fully human. So, in reality, asking this question to the disciples isn't strange at all. Jesus knows who He is, and He knows all that the disciples have seen and learned, but this question allows them to articulate for themselves what that means *to them.*

Jesus didn't go around announcing His credentials or making a big ceremony about His name or title. He just enters their lives, preaching the good news of His gospel of grace. He walks with them on the road, and He looks in their eyes as He listens to their questions. He heals the sick, gives dignity to the poor and the outcast, and spreads out an invitation to all to follow Him.

He spends His time *with* them, and rather than telling them who He is, *He just shows them.* And spending time in His presence—with Jesus—that is how their hearts recognize who He really is. It is only after Peter spends time getting to know Jesus that he is able to make his great confession. It takes *being with Jesus*, for Peter to be able to confess, "You are the Messiah, the Son of the living God." Before Peter steps into what will be his calling, there first must be a personal confession. *"You are the Messiah, the Son of the living God."*

And like Peter and the other disciples, Jesus asks us that same question today. "*Who do you say that I am?*" We can use words that we've heard other people say, and we can come up with an answer that we think He wants to hear, but that's not why Jesus asks questions, is it?

He is stirring up truth in our hearts, and showing us more and more of who He is every day. And just as it was with the disciples the day Jesus asked them this question, it doesn't matter as much what we've heard other people say about Jesus—*it matters who He has become to us.*

So, imagine, today that you are sitting there with Jesus. Imagine Him asking you the question— *"Who do you say that I am?"* Don't just tell Him what you think He wants to hear—that's not why He is asking. Even if you don't have it all figured out and even if there are still things you don't fully understand, tell Him what you *do* know. Tell Him all that is in your heart. He already knows, of course, but sometimes as we search our own hearts, and we speak out the truth we find there, we uncover what Jesus already knows but what we need to find out, for ourselves.

Jesus is still asking, "who do you say that I am?" So, how will you answer Him today? What will you tell Him? What is the confession of your heart today?

GATES OF HELL, CAESEREA PHILIPPI

13

[15] "But what about you?" he asked. "Who do you say I am?"

[16] Simon Peter answered, "You are the Messiah, the Son of the living God."

[17] Jesus replied, "Blessed are you, Simon son of Jonah, for this was not revealed to you by flesh and blood, but by my Father in heaven. [18] And I tell you that you are Peter, and on this rock I will build my church, and the gates of Hades will not overcome it.

Matthew 16:15-18 (NIV)

In Peter's life with Jesus, there are many significant moments, and the interaction in this passage displays one of the most significant moments of all.

Here, we see a profound exchange. In this moment, Peter becomes all that Jesus had already known he would be. And Jesus praises Peter for his answer. He takes this moment to call out what He sees in this fisherman, turned disciple who has been in the presence of Jesus and learned to hear from God. Jesus acknowledges that Peter's great confession of faith is not based on anything he has read or heard someone else say. Jesus affirms that Peter has heard from the heart of the Father, and his eyes have been opened to a deep spiritual revelation that didn't come from someone else's revelation, but from God, the Father Himself, right to the heart of Peter.

There is first a confession that then gives way to a calling. With his confession, Peter tells Jesus that he understands who He is. *And then, Jesus tells Peter who he is.*

"And I tell you that you are Peter, and on this rock, I will build my church…"

Jesus had once before told Simon that He would call him Peter, on the very first day they met. But that day, it was something that only Jesus could see—something that up until that point, had not yet been true. That day, years before, when Jesus had spoken those words, Peter had really only ever been Simon and had done nothing to earn the reputation of being "the Rock." But this day, after years of living and following Jesus, *Simon begins to look more like Peter*—more like what Jesus had spoken over him years before.

Jesus had already told him who he would be. But it had taken time in the presence of Jesus Himself for Simon to become the person Jesus had already known was there. This fisherman—this brother, son, husband, and friend—he is changed by the presence of Jesus. He begins to hear from God and is forever changed.

Simon, *with Jesus in him*, becomes Peter. Simon, the fisherman, transforms into Peter, the Rock. Peter's answer to Jesus' question reveals what had been born deep in his heart. And it causes Jesus to affirm back to Peter exactly who He says Peter to be. It is the Jesus *in him* and *with him* that allows Simon to rise up and step into his *new identity as Peter.*

His confession leads to his true calling. Because it is Jesus, in us, that makes us who we really are. This is an incredibly important moment in the life of Peter. It's significant, not because of what Peter himself brings or has to offer, but because of what the Father initiates and shares with him.

Jesus had once spoken a prophetic promise over Simon the fisherman. Here we start to see that take shape. Long before it had become a reality, Jesus had already known who Peter would become. And in the presence of Jesus and with the revelation of the Father's Covenant love, Simon gains his new identity in Jesus. *And with this new identity comes a new name. With his new name, a new mission.*

"And I tell you that you are Peter, and on this rock, I will build my church…"

It is Jesus that will do the building, and with Peter's confession of faith, Jesus invites Peter into this mission of building His Church. Jesus is the initiator and the completer of the Covenant with His people. It is Jesus that will do the work of bringing His Kingdom on earth. It is Jesus that builds up His Bride, the Church. Jesus is the One who will bring it to pass.

Jesus is the Cornerstone. And Peter, the Rock—the first to make this confession of faith—is the foundation stone of the Church that Jesus will build on the bedrock of all those believers who will confess their faith in Him.

And here, it's as if Jesus is saying, "Peter, this is who I say that you are. I call you not by what I see in front of me, but by who you are in the Father. I see you as you are *in Me* and what *I will do in you and through you.*"

Once again, we see the relationship between Jesus and Peter is very much a picture of the Father's heart toward us. The heart of God reaches out for each of us, offering us the opportunity to proclaim *who Jesus is to us* and to respond to who He is by following Him with our very lives. The heartbeat behind the message He gives to Peter is one that still echoes for us even today.

You will know yourself, as you are already known.
And because I am with you, you have a new name, and a new identity, and a new mission.
Not because of you, but because I am with you. Because of who I am and what I will do in your life.
My Covenant is greater than your commitment.
And because I am with you, you are free to know yourself as you are already known,
and rise up and be who I call you to be.

VALLEY BEFORE GALILLEE

14

²¹ From that time on Jesus began to explain to his disciples that he must go to Jerusalem and suffer many things at the hands of the elders, the chief priests and the teachers of the law, and that he must be killed and on the third day be raised to life.

²² Peter took him aside and began to rebuke him. "Never, Lord!" he said. "This shall never happen to you!"

²³ Jesus turned and said to Peter, "Get behind me, Satan! You are a stumbling block to me; you do not have in mind the concerns of God, but merely human concerns."

²⁴ Then Jesus said to his disciples, "Whoever wants to be my disciple must deny themselves and take up their cross and follow me. ²⁵ For whoever wants to save their life will lose it, but whoever loses their life for me will find it. ²⁶ What good will it be for someone to gain the whole world, yet forfeit their soul? Or what can anyone give in exchange for their soul? ²⁷ For the Son of Man is going to come in his Father's glory with his angels, and then he will reward each person according to what they have done.

²⁸ "Truly I tell you, some who are standing here will not taste death before they see the Son of Man coming in his kingdom."

Matthew 16: 21-28 (NIV)

It is the best of times, and then quickly, the worst of times. True to the character of Peter, this interaction is a clear picture of how one moment, all appears well, at a high point, in fact, but the next moment swings to a halting low.

Peter's profound confession of Christ has *just* taken place. The affirmation of Jesus is fresh on Peter's ears for communicating a spiritual revelation that he had received straight from the heart of the Father. Peter's confession of Jesus as the Messiah, the Son of God, leads to a crucial life-changing exchange between them. Peter tells Jesus that he understands who He really is, and in return, Jesus tells Peter who he really is. The words of Jesus back to Peter mark a significant moment as Jesus affirms Peter's new name and new identity. Jesus casts vision for His Kingdom come to earth and speaks blessing over the foundational role He chooses Peter to play. Jesus gives Peter a glowing stamp of approval and affirms the way He'll use him in the Kingdom.

But fairly quickly, the interaction takes an abrupt turn. Jesus begins to explain that, as Christ the Messiah, He must suffer and be killed before being raised to life on the third day. Peter, though, is not having it and responds in immediate protest! He actually *rebukes* Jesus. When he can't wrap his mind around this plan that Jesus is unfolding, he insists there must be a better way.

As it is for all of us, part of Peter's journey here is to understand the cross of Christ. And if we are to understand the cross of Christ at all, we have to come to terms with *the need* for the cross of Christ. It's understandable to question a plan that involves suffering and death. But a part of our own spiritual formation, just as it is a part of Peter's, is to understand the need for reconciliation between a sinful people and a Holy God. And for that, there must be atonement for sin. There must be a sacrifice that settles the debt and makes a way for restoration. Understanding *the true need for the Cross* comes only after a great journey of understanding our own sin in light of the perfect, unfathomable, sacrificial love of Christ.

It's hard to know what we would have done in that moment. As harsh as the interaction appears, Peter's response, voicing confusion and unbelief, is understandable, isn't it? This is *the first time* that Peter and the other disciples are hearing Jesus speak so directly about what is to come. Understandably, Peter is confused and fearful as he voices a desire for things to go another way. Who among us would want to see someone we love suffer?

In seasons of pain, or confusion, or even suffering, we can reflect on what is happening in our lives or in the lives of those we love, and it can be easy to assume something is wrong or that the ship is off course. Instead of leaning in and listening closely to the heart of the Father, it can be easy to think, "surely this isn't God's plan." Suffering, pain, and grief give way to our soul's deep desire for a different outcome. We may not actually rebuke God with the words from our mouths, but we can certainly take on the heart of Peter when things get hard. It is easy to associate suffering or pain with something that is wrong and needs to be fixed.

Like Peter, we can find ourselves believing God fully in one moment and then doubting His plan and His ways the next. We may or may not *rebuke* Him with our words, but we can certainly lean more toward the ways of the world, tempting us with comfort and security, rather than leaning toward the ways of God. Especially if that road involves discomfort or insecurity.

The response of Jesus to Peter in that moment may feel harsh at first, but with further investigation, the words that Jesus chooses, begin to make a little more sense. Jesus is both Divine in nature and also human—the Word made flesh, Immanuel, God with us. Jesus, Himself had been the target of the enemy trying to tempt Him to abandon God's plan when things got tough. At the beginning of Jesus' public ministry, it says in Matthew 4, "He was led by the Spirit into the wilderness to be tempted by the devil." The way the enemy tried to entice Jesus was by tempting Him with a way that was easier when hunger and humility brought pain and discomfort. The enemy didn't try to tempt Jesus with anything obviously sinful or wicked. The method of the enemy was simply to dangle an easier way—to offer comfort, ease, a simple path of least resistance, and instant relief. So, there is history underneath the strong words of Jesus as He says to Peter,

"Get behind me, Satan! You are a stumbling block to me; you do not have in mind the concerns of God, but merely human concerns."

He speaks those words with a voice of experience. Jesus has been the target of the enticing schemes of the enemy. And He recognizes the plan of the enemy to cause doubt in the heart of a believer when the sovereign plan of God seems like an uphill journey filled with pain, suffering, and hardship. Maybe it's not Peter himself He is speaking to, but to the possibility within Peter— the possibility that is also within each of us—to choose the concerns of our own selves rather than the concerns of God.

We are probably all familiar with that temptation. When God's plan leads us down a road of confusion, pain, longing, even suffering, we can easily be tempted to shift the course, and choose comfort above all else. In his book, *When God's Ways Make No Sense,* Larry Crabb says that when Christians experience a season when God's thoughts and ways make no sense to us, we are confronted with three options. We can resist and run, we can distort and deny, or we can tremble and trust.

He says, "When we realize that God's way of running the world and guiding our lives make no sense, *tremble.* Tremble before a God whose thoughts and ways are far above our thoughts and ways about what the truly good life is and how to live it. Feel our confusion. Own our doubts. Embrace our fears. Face our disappointment. Experience our anguish. Then *trust…*

Tremble before the incomprehensible God and trust that He is good. Trust that His love is committed to our growing awareness of the deepest and happiest well-being that's available to us now, that His love will lead us into an eternity where we will know every delight we were created to enjoy. Gaze on the cross. Remember Christ's death. Nowhere is the love of the incomprehensible God more fully and clearly displayed. But always remember: tastes now, the full banquet later. Tremble before what our eyes can see and our hearts can feel. Trust in what our faith can believe, that the longed-for satisfaction of our deepest thirst lies ahead."[1]

Jesus is leading Peter and the disciples down the narrow road of the Kingdom, and they don't fully understand it, yet. But Jesus is giving them a guardrail, as they walk the narrow path. The heart of Jesus' message here is clear…in the Kingdom of God, *hard doesn't necessarily equal wrong.* A journey filled with opposition, pain, suffering, confusion, sorrow, or even death, does not necessarily equal a journey that is off course. As always, the ways of the Kingdom are upside-down, and the Sovereignty of God often works in ways we cannot see or understand. To us, what looks like death, might simply be the path to new life. What we perceive to be punishment or pruning might actually be provision and protection. The temptation comes when we stop listening to the Father's voice and listen instead to the tempting voices offering comfort, ease, relief, answers, security, the path of least resistance, or even happiness over the deep abiding work of choosing the Father's will above our own.

The enemy and the ways of this world will always be there enticing us with the possibility of comfort. That voice of temptation will always try to distract us from hearing the Father's voice, but the words of Jesus draw us back to the heart of the Father. His voice, echoing for us again, that *hard doesn't necessarily mean wrong*, and that God is always working in the greater story in ways we cannot see. Like Peter, we may hear that voice clearly one minute but be enticed by our own affections for the ways of the world in the next. But there is always an opportunity to tremble, and yet also, to trust. And just as He did for Peter, the voice of Jesus is always calling us back to Himself, offering the invitation to take up our cross and follow Him, right down the narrow road that leads to life.

MT. TABOR

15

28 Some eight days after these sayings, He took along Peter and John and James, and went up on the mountain to pray. 29 And while He was praying, the appearance of His face became different, and His clothing became white and gleaming. 30 And behold, two men were talking with Him; and they were Moses and Elijah, 31 who, appearing in glory, were speaking of His departure which He was about to accomplish at Jerusalem.

32 Now Peter and his companions had been overcome with sleep; but when they were fully awake, they saw His glory and the two men standing with Him. 33 And as these were leaving Him, Peter said to Jesus, "Master, it is good for us to be here; let us make three tabernacles: one for You, and one for Moses, and one for Elijah"—not realizing what he was saying. 34 While he was saying this, a cloud formed and began to overshadow them; and they were afraid as they entered the cloud. 35 Then a voice came out of the cloud, saying, "This is My Son, My Chosen One; listen to Him!" 36 And when the voice had spoken, Jesus was found alone. And they kept silent, and reported to no one in those days any of the things which they had seen.

Luke 9:28-36 (NASB)

Sometimes Jesus pulls back the curtain and gives us a glimpse of the heavenly and miraculous right in the middle of our own ordinary lives. That is certainly what Jesus does for Peter here, along with James and John, at the Transfiguration. Peter and the other disciples have been walking with Jesus for some time, and although they are learning and growing, it's possible they don't truly understand fully who Jesus is, as the Son of God, and what is up ahead on the road for Him.

Scripture tell us they "went up on the mountain to pray." The name of the mountain isn't given, though some commentators believe it to be Mt. Tabor, while others think this encounter happened on Mt. Hermon.[1] We do know that Peter experiences this secret and sacred encounter, getting a glimpse of the true power and might in the Kingdom of God, as he hears from God Himself, who Jesus is.

Having grown up in the Jewish tradition, Peter would have studied "the Law and the Prophets." These servants of God—Moses, and Elijah—were the most revered among all the Old Testament figures. Moses, the Great Lawgiver, personified *the Law*, and Elijah, the quintessential Old Testament Prophet, personified *the Prophets*.[2] Peter's first response as he witnesses the two men talking with Jesus, "appearing in glory" is awe, reverence, and possibly shock. But an important distinction is made here. Peter is trying to make sense of it all, and it says, "while he was saying this, a cloud formed and began to overshadow them." The voice of God speaks, and He points not to the three, *but to Jesus, alone.*

Throughout the Old Testament, all of history has pointed to Jesus and culminates in His coming to His people as Immanuel, God With Us, the Messiah, and Anointed One. So to see Jesus, transfigured in front of them, His face shining like the sun alongside Moses and Elijah, marks an important moment in the story of God. As integral as Moses had been to the story of God, he still spoke of the One who was coming. And while Elijah's part in the story was significant as well, he, too, spoke of the One who would come later. Peter sees before him two of the pillars of faith, Moses, and Elijah, talking to Jesus. But Peter also fully sees *Jesus* with his own eyes, as He is transformed, and His face changes, and His clothes become dazzling white. Much is written about the response of Peter as he reacts in this moment, "not realizing what he was saying."

After witnessing something like that, who could even find words? Much less words that appropriately articulate and comprehend what you're seeing? Surely Peter is stunned. Maybe he is a verbal processor or a nervous talker. It's certainly possible that Peter doesn't grasp the fullness of what he is seeing at first, but the voice of God, Himself, brings clarity to a moment that must certainly feel like a dream.

> **"This is My Son, My Chosen One; listen to Him!" And when the voice had spoken, Jesus was found alone.**

In the story of God, after earlier chapters had paved the way, and the prophets of old had foretold of His coming, even God the Father, points to Jesus alone. This encounter is one of only two times in the Synoptic Gospels that *God speaks*. The first is in Luke 3:21-22 when Jesus is baptized. This is the second. In both cases, God speaks of His beloved Son, Jesus. And on the top of the mountain, God speaks about His Son with a call to *listen to Him.*

That day on the top of the mountain, held many profound and life-changing moments. *Peter bears witness to this significant moment in time where the whole story of God is illuminated in the radiance of Jesus Christ.* Jesus invites Peter into the intimacy of His communion with the Father, and Peter is able to bear witness to the Father's heart about His Son. In hearing God's Word, Jesus allows Peter to see behind the curtain of His own humanity and witness the miraculous, hearing God Himself say, *"This is My Son, My Chosen One. Listen to Him."* Peter sees that once the voice of God has spoken, *it is Jesus alone who is left standing.* This has to deepen Peter's understanding of who Jesus really is. Not only does he see with greater depth who Jesus is to the Father, but he sees who Jesus is to the rest of us—God's Chosen One who had been foretold for generations. And as significant as the great chapters of the story of God had been thus far, the ultimate deliverance of God's people wouldn't come through Moses or Elijah. The true restoration and redemption of

God's people would be found *in Jesus, alone.* That day on the mountaintop, Jesus holds back the curtain and gives us all a glimpse into the miraculous, powerful, holy, and sacred Kingdom of God. Just as it had been for Moses and Elijah, Jesus brings Peter to the mountaintop, inviting him to an eye-opening, life-changing encounter with God Himself.

Sometimes God is working in the larger story of the Kingdom of God in ways we cannot see or understand. And sometimes He opens our eyes to see and to know Him in ways we never have before. We get a glimpse into the holy mysteries of Christ from this mountaintop experience. One of the breadcrumb trails from our ancient Scripture in the Old Testament leads us to an incredible epiphany here in this passage in the New Testament. During his lifetime, Moses never made it to the Promised Land. But now, here he stands on the top of a mountain and in the presence of a radiant Jesus, looking toward the ultimate and final deliverance of God's people. And perhaps, the most important revelation of all is that in all history, all creation, all who have gone before in the history of God—*it all culminates in the person of Jesus.*

We have the benefit of this holy and sacred encounter recorded in the Gospels—an encounter Jesus told Peter, James, and John to tell no one about until He'd been raised to life at the Resurrection. There is no way to know what it was truly like that day on the mountaintop, seeing, with your own eyes Jesus transfigured right before you and hearing the voice of God with your own ears.

What we do know, is that it forever changes Peter's journey of transformation. Matthew 17 also describes what Peter witnesses at the Transfiguration and actually gives us some good perspective about his journey. In the original language, the word used in Matthew 17 to describe Jesus as "transfigured" is actually from the Greek word, *metamorphoó*, which means "to transform."[3] The use of this particular word here is not surprising, because it paints the picture of what happens to Jesus as He changes physically in those moments on the mountaintop. What's interesting is that this same original Greek word is used in Romans 12:2, which says, "And do not be conformed to this world, but be *transformed* by the renewing of your mind, so that you may prove what the will of God is, that which is good and acceptable and perfect."

Peter is one of only three people who are brought into this secret and sacred moment to witness Jesus undergo a physical transformation in front of them. Ironically, Peter is undergoing his own metamorphosis as well, but his transformation isn't anything that could be seen from the outside. Peter's soul is on a journey of transformation as he grows and changes while following Jesus. Throughout their time together so far, Jesus has continued to pastor the soul of Peter on his journey of spiritual formation, just as Jesus does with each of us, as we are on our own journey of faith.

Years and years later, toward the end of his life, Peter would tell us in his own words what that day was like and how he saw prophecy fulfilled and confirmed in the life of Jesus, challenging us to open our eyes in the same way.

> **[16] For we did not follow cleverly contrived myths when we made known to you the power and coming of our Lord Jesus Christ; instead, we were eyewitnesses of his majesty. [17] For he received honor and glory from God the Father when the voice came to him from the Majestic Glory, saying "This is my beloved Son, with whom I am well-pleased!" [18] We ourselves heard this voice when it came from heaven while we were with him on the holy mountain. [19] We also have the prophetic word strongly confirmed, and you will do well to pay attention to it, as to a lamp shining in a dark place, until the day dawns and the morning star rises in your hearts. (2 Peter 1:16-19 CSB)**

MOUNTAINS NEAR GALILEE

16

²⁷Then Peter said to Him, "Behold, we have left everything and followed You; what then will there be for us?"

Matthew 19:27 (NASB)

At this point in the relationship between Jesus and the disciples, we often see Peter asking questions that reflect many of the mysteries that come along with a life of faith in Jesus.

We can identify with that. We too, can understand what it's like to have made a decision to follow Jesus, but to still not understand fully what that means. As we read these encounters in Scripture, we are given a glimpse of what it's like for Peter to walk with Jesus. We can see the progression of his transformation as he follows Jesus *but still has questions.* His choice to follow Jesus is clear. But the journey is far from over, and while Peter has been able to witness great signs and wonders, he is still on the long journey of his own soul's formation, in light of Christ.

Peter is in the messy middle of transformation. He is learning, growing, and undoubtedly being marked by the life and teaching of Jesus, and we get to listen in as he *continues to ask honest questions.* If we look closely, we might even be able to see ourselves in some of the interactions of the disciples. They are still trying to wrap their minds around the teachings of Jesus and just what it means to follow Him. They ask honest questions of Jesus that might echo some of the deep questions we sometimes have in our own hearts, even if we never actually articulate them. Jesus continues to welcome their questions, often speaking back to them in parables, reframing their conversation and giving them a new lens through which they can view all that is stirring deep in their hearts.

In Matthew 18 and 19, we come upon several passages when the disciples come to Jesus with questions. In Matthew 18:1 they ask Jesus,

"Who then is the greatest in the kingdom of heaven?"

Instead of answering, or even reprimanding what may be at the root of the question, Jesus responds by calling over a child.

"Truly I tell you," He said, "unless you turn and become like children, you will never enter the kingdom of heaven. Therefore, whoever humbles himself like this child—this one is the greatest in the kingdom of heaven."

Jesus continues to turn everything they'd ever known upside-down. He teaches that it is not the qualities of personal ambition, wealth, prestige, or position that show greatness in the Kingdom of God. Instead, it is the posture of coming to God with childlike faith and humility that has value in the Kingdom of Heaven. Later in Matthew 18:21, we read this exchange between Peter and Jesus.

Then Peter approached him and asked, "Lord, how many times shall I forgive my brother or sister who sins against me? As many as seven times?" "I tell you, not as many as seven," Jesus replied, "but seventy times seven."

It's noteworthy that it is *Peter* who asks Jesus a question about forgiveness. There is a bit of foreshadowing and a few crumbs on the breadcrumb trail that Jesus is leaving for Peter about the ways of love and forgiveness in the Kingdom of God. On this occasion, Peter may think that he is being very generous in his own estimation of how often he should forgive.

Already, Jesus is planting a seed that in the upside-down Kingdom of heaven, the forgiveness of God is incomprehensible to the human heart and mind. It extends lavishly beyond what the human heart could offer on its own.

We learn a lot about the nature of Jesus in the way that those closest to Him feel comfortable asking Him open and honest questions—even if those questions reveal a more selfish or prideful side of the one asking.

Just a short time later in Matthew 19, Jesus is teaching the familiar parable that "it is easier for a camel to go through the eye of a needle, than for a rich man to enter the kingdom of God." The disciples are astonished, and their confusion leads to more questions. Matthew 19, verse 27 tells us that it is Peter who speaks up.

Then Peter responded to him, "See, we have left everything and followed you. So what will there be for us?"

You've got to love the guts and the honesty of Peter. He's the guy who actually asks the question that everyone else is undoubtedly thinking. His question would be easy to reprimand, but one that is much better brought into the light with an honest discussion about the deeper things stirring beneath the surface. As usual, the answers Jesus gives are not simple or straightforward, but rather an invitation for the listener to engage personally with the truth He is teaching. The words of Jesus remind us again how the ways of His Kingdom are not at all like the ways of the world.

"But many who are first will be last, and many who are last will be first." (Matthew 19:30 NIV)

What a gift to be able to witness the authentic friendship between Jesus and Peter. What a privilege to see the gentle but firm way that Jesus continues to engage Peter, asking him questions and responding to Peter's own questions in a way that brings truth to light and draws hearts back to Himself.

These passages serve as a great reminder that, just as He did for Peter, *Jesus welcomes our honest questions and our deep wrestling. He is present with us on each and every step of our own journey of transformation.*

PATHWAY IN THE OLD CITY, JERUSALEM

17

[7] Then came the day of Unleavened Bread on which the Passover lamb had to be sacrificed. [8] Jesus sent Peter and John, saying, "Go and make preparations for us to eat the Passover."

[9] "Where do you want us to prepare for it?" they asked.

[10] He replied, "As you enter the city, a man carrying a jar of water will meet you. Follow him to the house that he enters, [11] and say to the owner of the house, 'The Teacher asks: Where is the guest room, where I may eat the Passover with my disciples?' [12] He will show you a large room upstairs, all furnished. Make preparations there."

[13] They left and found things just as Jesus had told them. So they prepared the Passover.

[14] When the hour came, Jesus and his apostles reclined at the table. [15] And he said to them, "I have eagerly desired to eat this Passover with you before I suffer. [16] For I tell you, I will not eat it again until it finds fulfillment in the kingdom of God."

Luke 22:7-16 (NIV)

Can you picture exactly what your home is like on Christmas morning? If you close your eyes, can you imagine the familiar scene? What sights, and sounds, and smells would you find if you were to walk in the room right now? Holidays can have a funny way of making a brand new day feel already familiar, almost as if we've lived it before. Even if some of the elements change from year to year, many things stay the same. Maybe you eat the same thing for breakfast every Christmas morning. Maybe you have a tradition of how the order of the morning unfolds. Maybe you place a Christmas tree at the same place in the room each year or hang the same stockings by the chimney with care. We all have those things that happen over and over each year at the holidays. It can almost feel like deja-vu because we've participated in the practice so many times before.

That is what the Passover would have been like for Jesus and the disciples. They'd grown up in the Jewish tradition so the Feast of Passover was a set of days marked on the calendar that they visited over and over, each and every year. It probably felt as familiar to them, as their own reflections in a mirror.

This year as the day approaches, the disciples find themselves anticipating this familiar celebration in Jerusalem with their brothers in Christ rather than with their families at home. Having observed the Feast of Passover and the annual Seder dinner every year of their lives, the disciples probably thought they knew exactly what to expect on an evening like this. Jesus gives Peter and John the task of preparing the familiar Passover dinner. He had already gone before them and told them exactly what to look for and where they could begin their preparations. As is the way of Jesus, He'd already anticipated their needs and had made arrangements beforehand. And when Peter and John take on the task Jesus had given them, they find things *exactly as He said they would be.*

Peter and John had been doing this their whole lives, and because of that, they know exactly how to arrange the room and set the low, reclining table. They know exactly what food and drink need to be prepared and placed on the table so the traditional re-telling of the Passover story can take place.

Year after year, the disciples had gathered with their loved ones to remember and re-tell the story of how long ago, the people of God were held captive as slaves by the Pharaoh in Egypt. During that bitterly difficult season, they prayed for God to rescue them. Each of the elements of the Passover Seder meal—each bite of food and each drink on the table—served as a way to remember and tell a part of the story of the first Passover.

The word *Seder* is actually translated as "order."[1] By observing "the order" of the Passover Feast, families would tell of God's faithfulness as He rescued His people from slavery. They'd remember when the blood of the Passover lamb was spread across the doorframe of their homes, and the people of God were spared death and led out of captivity into freedom. Each year, the people of God would gather and read the Scriptures and together, sing songs that gave an offering of thanks and praise in remembrance of God's faithfulness. Each word that was spoken, each bite of food eaten, each prayer offered together in unison, would all collectively point to God's great redemption story and how He a made a way for His people to walk in freedom.

It is particularly noteworthy that Jesus gives Peter and John the job of preparing for their Seder dinner and Passover Feast. It is a job that could have easily been done by a servant. But by having Peter and John make the preparations, and set the table for the others, Jesus is allowing them to take on the role of a servant to their brothers. By allowing them to set the table, Jesus Himself is actually setting the table for a Passover unlike any they had ever known.

As they sit down to something so familiar, they can't yet know that *this* Seder meal, *this* Feast of Passover, will become *the Last Supper*. They don't yet know that Jesus, whom John the Baptist had called *"the Lamb of God,"* is about to fulfill the Scriptures they'd known their whole lives. Jesus says to them—

**"I have eagerly desired to eat this Passover with you before I suffer. For I tell you,
I will not eat it again until it finds fulfillment in the kingdom of God."**

This evening together would become their last. Jesus will use the re-telling of the Passover story to teach them about His New Covenant and how He'd come to bring the redemption of the people of God forever through His own perfect sacrifice.

The very words they'd been saying their whole lives become real that night in the words of Jesus Himself. And though everything is familiar, it would never again be the same. Jesus is going to use something that they'd been doing their whole lives, *to change the rest of their lives forever.*

ANCIENT CELLAR IN ISRAEL

18

¹It was just before the Passover Festival. Jesus knew that the hour had come for him to leave this world and go to the Father. Having loved his own who were in the world, he loved them to the end.

²The evening meal was in progress, and the devil had already prompted Judas, the son of Simon Iscariot, to betray Jesus. ³Jesus knew that the Father had put all things under his power, and that he had come from God and was returning to God; ⁴so he got up from the meal, took off his outer clothing, and wrapped a towel around his waist. ⁵After that, he poured water into a basin and began to wash his disciples' feet, drying them with the towel that was wrapped around him.

⁶He came to Simon Peter, who said to him, "Lord, are you going to wash my feet?"

⁷Jesus replied, "You do not realize now what I am doing, but later you will understand."

⁸"No," said Peter, "you shall never wash my feet."

Jesus answered, "Unless I wash you, you have no part with me."

⁹"Then, Lord," Simon Peter replied, "not just my feet but my hands and my head as well!"

¹⁰Jesus answered, "Those who have had a bath need only to wash their feet; their whole body is clean. And you are clean, though not every one of you." ¹¹For he knew who was going to betray him, and that was why he said not every one was clean.

¹²When he had finished washing their feet, he put on his clothes and returned to his place. "Do you understand what I have done for you?" he asked them. ¹³"You call me 'Teacher' and 'Lord,' and rightly so, for that is what I am. ¹⁴Now that I, your Lord and Teacher, have washed your feet, you also should wash one another's feet. ¹⁵I have set you an example that you should do as I have done for you. ¹⁶Very truly I tell you, no servant is greater than his master, nor is a messenger greater than the one who sent him. ¹⁷Now that you know these things, you will be blessed if you do them.

John 13:1-17 (NIV)

The evening that would become *the Last Supper* is so prolific, and Jesus fills it with so many gospel truths and so many breadcrumbs that it is worth a closer look on our journey together. The first place we'll look together is to Jesus, Himself. There are famous iconic works of art that depict this evening, but none paint a more authentic portrait of Jesus than His own words and actions. If we cannot take our eyes off of Jesus, it is for good reason. And like when we look upon any iconic masterpiece, to fully appreciate each masterful stroke, it can be helpful to know the background and context that illuminate each intricate detail.

There would have been many familiar elements to the evening for Peter and the other disciples, but understandably, they are confused when Jesus takes this moment and goes off script. And there *is* actually a script in a traditional Passover Seder. It is customary to follow the *hagaddah*, which gives the order of events for the traditional words and prayers as they are spoken aloud together throughout the evening.[1]

But after the traditional moment set apart for the washing of hands, Scripture describes what happens next.

> "…He poured water into a basin and began to wash his disciples' feet, drying them with the towel that was wrapped around him."

This moment where Jesus goes "off script" paints a perfect picture of His character. The words at the beginning of the thirteenth chapter of John's Gospel say it perfectly.

> **Jesus knew that the hour had come for him to leave this world and go to the Father. Having loved his own who were in the world, he loved them to the end.**

Jesus knows it is their last evening together, and despite the pain and suffering He already knows He is about to endure, as the evening begins, His thoughts are for his brothers. And *He loves them to the end.*

He chooses this moment to serve them and show His great love in a way that catches them off guard. It isn't uncommon for feet to be washed, as the traditional sandals worn at this time would often cause feet to gather dirt. But the washing of feet is a task usually performed by a servant.

Jesus—their rabbi, teacher, and leader—holds the unspoken title of the greatest among them. Yet He chooses this moment to take on the role of the servant. He kneels before each of them, one at a time, and gently and lovingly washes away the dirt, grime, and stench their feet had dragged in. He then carefully dries their feet with the towel He'd gathered at His waist.

It is probably an unsettling experience for them. They'd probably had their feet washed hundreds of times before on an evening like this. But on this night, Jesus, Himself is on His knees in front of them doing something a servant would usually do. *He is serving them.*

Peter can't handle it. It doesn't feel right. He doesn't understand. He had once kneeled at the feet of Jesus, overwhelmingly humbled and so aware of His own sin and brokenness in light of the Holiness of Jesus. He can't reconcile now, how in this moment—in the middle of a night that should go precisely like all the nights before—Jesus is on *His* knees, kneeling before them, washing their feet like a servant.

It isn't the first time that Peter doesn't understand the words or the way of Jesus. It isn't the first time that being in the presence of Jesus means his eyes are seeing something that his heart and his mind can't comprehend. Peter had seen Jesus walk on water, heal the sick, and raise a dead body back to life. He'd seen Jesus transfigured before him in radiant light. It isn't the first time that Peter can't believe his eyes, and it isn't the first time that he nervously mumbles something out loud, trying to make sense of it.

At first, Peter protests. "No, you shall never wash my feet." Jesus responds by saying "Unless I wash you, you have no part with me." It's almost as if Jesus is saying, "Peter, if you are going to be too proud to let me do this for you, you'll miss everything." And in hearing the response of Jesus, Peter swings all the way to the other side, thinking, *in that case,* he should offer himself to be washed head to toe.

Peter doesn't understand, at first. And to be fair, who among us would?

There has never been a man like Jesus before. There has never been someone as wise, as powerful, as all-knowing and inviting as Jesus has been. But instead of sitting in a place of prestige, waiting to be honored for His many praiseworthy qualities, He kneels down to serve them. Instead of taking His place as the guest of honor that He truly is, He takes the position of host, having prepared the way for the evening and then guiding them through each part. Instead of reclining and being waited on, He is the most active one at the table, taking the towel Himself, serving them and washing their feet.

This exchange between Jesus and Peter—and what happens tangibly and physically—is really a reflection of the heart shift that must happen spiritually. Peter can't wrap his head around this extravagant act of Jesus. It seems unspeakable that someone of His position, His power, His holiness would lower Himself to serve in this way.

But that is a picture of the gospel, isn't it? Jesus, Himself left heaven to come to earth as Immanuel, God with us, to give us the gift of eternal life in and through Him. It's a gift that is undeserved and almost too much to comprehend. And on this night, Jesus is showing Peter and the disciples the gospel of His grace in action. As Jesus lowers to His knees to wash Peter's feet, Peter cannot understand it and questions Him. Jesus responds by saying "You do not realize now what I am doing, but later you will understand." Jesus is speaking in the present to the way He is washing their feet, but also to the way He is giving His very life for them.

The words of Jesus here are an invitation for Peter to surrender and trust Jesus and what He is doing, even if he doesn't understand it just yet. Jesus doesn't give Peter all the answers. Instead, He continues moving forward in love and positions Peter to simply surrender to it.

But Peter remains unsure and struggles to let Jesus continue. For Peter to begin to comprehend and receive the gift, there must be a posture of humility. There must be an acknowledgment of how greatly undeserved the sacrifice of love given on his behalf really is. Only then, when he understands that, will he be positioned to receive it.

Jesus doesn't want Peter to miss it. He gives Peter the opportunity to surrender in humility to letting Jesus wash his feet. He gives Peter a chance to shift the posture of his heart to humbly receive the incomprehensible saving grace of Jesus deep in his soul. On this night, with the towel and the basin, Jesus isn't just teaching Peter His gospel. He is living it right before him.

And just as it was for Peter that night, it is a journey that each of our souls must make if we are to have any part with Jesus. There must be an acknowledgment, made in great humility that anything Jesus does on our behalf is truly unmerited and undeserved. And yet, He does it still. Only in lowering ourselves, can we rightly see our great need for Jesus and the longing for rescue and redemption that only He can give. Incredible spiritual formation happens in us when we recognize that *we genuinely are unworthy* to have Jesus wash our feet, but in His posture of grace, He kneels before us and washes them even still. Once that realization begins to take root in us, only then can the gospel of His great love and grace come alive in us. Even if we don't understand it all just yet, the way forward to be with Jesus comes only in a posture of surrender. Only then can the unworthy soul begin to feel its worth in Christ alone.

ENTRANCE TO THE JAFFA GATE, THE OLD CITY, JERUSALEM

19

[14] When the hour came, Jesus and his apostles reclined at the table. [15] And he said to them, "I have eagerly desired to eat this Passover with you before I suffer. [16] For I tell you, I will not eat it again until it finds fulfillment in the kingdom of God."

[17] After taking the cup, he gave thanks and said, "Take this and divide it among you. [18] For I tell you I will not drink again from the fruit of the vine until the kingdom of God comes."

[19] And he took bread, gave thanks and broke it, and gave it to them, saying, "This is my body given for you; do this in remembrance of me."

[20] In the same way, after the supper he took the cup, saying, "This cup is the new covenant in my blood, which is poured out for you."

Luke 22: 14-20 (NIV)

It's been said that "from a Jewish perspective, *theology is not only taught, it is also eaten.*"[1] It's customary in the Jewish tradition to take part in the Seder meal during Passover, which incorporates the retelling of Exodus and God's deliverance from bondage in Egypt. Each element of the Seder meal and the Feast of Passover helped to re-tell God's great rescue story. In fact, Scripture in Deuteronomy 16:3 says that the Passover should be observed: "in order that you remember…"

Not only did each element of food and drink on the table tell the story of the history of God's people, but it also taught, experientially, many aspects of the faith. Each element on the table—the lamb, the bread, the wine—all held great significance. The retelling of the story every year was a reminder of God's heart for rescue and redemption, and the need for an imperfect people to make a way to a perfect God. Their whole lives at Passover, the people of God would remember how a blood sacrifice was the only way to cover over and make atonement for sin. And each year, a perfect lamb—one without spot or blemish—would be offered as a sacrifice, and its blood as an offering for the forgiveness of sin.

That night in the Upper Room at the Last Supper, Peter and the other disciples gather for what seems like just another yearly, traditional Passover meal. *Little did they know that Jesus is about to change everything.*

Jesus takes something that they'd known their whole lives and uses it to give them eyes to see who He really is and what He'd come to do. Jesus uses each of the elements of the Feast of Passover to show them how *He would be the fulfillment of it all.*

The sacrifice of a perfect, spotless lamb represented a way to cover over their sin and be reconciled to a Holy God. Under the Old Law, if sin was present, the only path to redemption came through sacrifice. We have not lived under the Law, and have no reference for the constant longing to be reconciled to God by making sacrifices. It might sound unusual for us today, but at this point in the story of God's people…making sacrifices, in an attempt to receive forgiveness, was all they had ever known. And here, Jesus uses the significance of Passover, and the lamb that was sacrificed each year for the forgiveness of sin, to give them eyes to see the greater story.

Years before, at the very beginning of Jesus' public ministry, John the Baptist had been making the way for the Lord. He was preaching, and teaching, and baptizing in God's name. John 1:29 says, "…he saw Jesus coming toward him and declared, 'Here is *the Lamb of God* who takes away the sin of the world!'" And again in John 1:35, John the Baptist calls Jesus *"the Lamb of God."*

Jesus is the Lamb of God and the One who came to take away the sin of the world, once and for all!

Later, the book of Revelation would reference "the Lamb." And even the Apostle Paul would one day refer to Jesus in this way in I Corinthians 5:7, saying "for indeed, you are clean because Christ, our Passover Lamb, has been sacrificed for us."

As the evening moves on, Jesus takes other elements on the table at the Passover meal and uses them to show how He is the fulfillment of the Law and how He will offer Himself to be the perfect sacrifice once and for all. Jesus takes the bread and the wine, two elements that had always been an important part of the Passover meal. He holds them and speaks to the disciples as He introduces His New Covenant. In what must have been a truly sacred moment, Jesus takes the unleavened bread—a picture of a life without sin—and breaks it before them. With that seemingly simple act, He is giving them new eyes to see something they'd seen their whole lives. He is transforming it into something new right before them.

As they watch Him hold the bread, did they think back on the time that He'd told them *He was the Bread of Life?* As they sit together around the table, do they feel the moment when everything shifts? In the way that only He can, Jesus is taking the traditions of the past and making all things new. He *is* the fulfillment of all that the Scriptures had always foretold, and He is making a way back to the heart of the Father forever, by introducing His New Covenant. *Only a few hours before Jesus willingly surrenders Himself to be arrested, beaten, and crucified to death, He offers these sacred words—*

"This is my body given for you; do this in remembrance of me." In the same way, after the supper he took the cup, saying, "This cup is the new covenant in my

blood, which is poured out for you."

And we begin to recognize with greater clarity that this moment, right here, when Jesus institutes His New Covenant, *is the origin of our sacrament of Communion.*

The people of God had always known the words of the great prophet Jeremiah, and how he foretold that one day, God would establish a New Covenant with His people. And right there at the table that night, the words of Jeremiah 31:31-33 were coming to life right before their eyes.

> [31]Behold, days are coming, declares the Lord, "when I will make a new covenant with the house of Israel and with the house of Judah, [32]not like the covenant I made with their fathers in the day I took them by the hand to bring them out of Egypt…my covenant that they broke, although I was a husband to them… [33]But this covenant…I will put my law within them, and on their heart I will write it; and I will be their God, and they shall be my people."

Jesus has come to change it all. We are no longer bound by the Old Law, and we no longer need to strive to offer sacrifices to be made right with God. Just as clearly as Jesus spoke to Peter and the other disciples that night in the Upper Room, Jesus is speaking these words of truth to us. He is offering Himself as the sacrifice for sin, and He is establishing His New Covenant. Sin has always separated people from a Holy God. But God loved us so much, that while we were yet sinners, Christ died for us![2] *His Covenant is greater than our commitment to Him!* What's different about the New Covenant is the way in which it is kept. God, through His perfect son, Jesus, establishes it, initiates it with us, and then *He also completes it!* He wanted so much to be with us that He gave us this New Covenant. He initiated the Covenant and covered over the cavern that had separated us to keep the Covenant, as well. And Jesus is using this moment at the Last Supper in the Upper Room to explain it to His closest followers. The way that Jesus prepares their hearts that night is so meaningful. Knowing what Jesus is about to willingly step into makes His Words all the more powerful. The sinless, spotless lamb is offering Himself as a perfect sacrifice. Out of His great love for us, He gives Himself to die for us. Because our commitment to Him, would never be enough, He gives us a New Covenant, made perfect by His perfect love.

When we participate in the Lord's Supper and Communion, we may hear someone say those words of Jesus…"*This is my body given for you; do this in remembrance of me…This cup is the new covenant in my blood, which is poured out for you.*"

When we realize the richness and deep symbolism that Jesus is offering as He holds the bread and the wine, we can see it so much more clearly now. When we understand the history and what the elements would have meant in *the past*, it gives such sacred meaning to what they mean *now and forever more.* Just as everything is changed forever for Peter and the other disciples that night, these words of Jesus take on new meaning for us as well, as we receive them with greater understanding.

The people of God in the past had always remembered His great deliverance through the Passover meal. Now in the New Covenant, Jesus invites us to remember His perfect and final sacrifice, and our own deliverance through the Lord's Supper.

Jesus is the Passover Lamb, and the perfect sacrifice, taking our place, bringing forgiveness for sin, and offering complete redemption once and for all.

And Jesus, the Bread of Life, is leaving the holiest of breadcrumb trails that had been winding through the generations, now leading right back to Himself as He prepares a feast at the greatest banqueting table of them all.

OLD CITY WALLS, JERUSALEM

20

²⁴ And there arose also a dispute among them as to which one of them was regarded to be greatest. ²⁵ And He said to them, "The kings of the Gentiles lord it over them; and those who have authority over them are called 'Benefactors.' ²⁶ But it is not this way with you, but the one who is the greatest among you must become like the youngest, and the leader like the servant. ²⁷ For who is greater, the one who reclines at the table or the one who serves? Is it not the one who reclines at the table? But I am among you as the one who serves.

²⁸ "You are those who have stood by Me in My trials; ²⁹ and just as My Father has granted Me a kingdom, I grant you ³⁰ that you may eat and drink at My table in My kingdom, and you will sit on thrones judging the twelve tribes of Israel."

Luke 22:24-30 (NASB)

It is an interesting time and place for the disciples to argue who among them is considered "the greatest." For a moment, these men sound less like chosen disciples sitting at the feet of Jesus and more like toddlers. Jesus is likely trying to facilitate what will be one of their most important and significant evenings together. He has to stop, however, and have a teachable moment about humility and serving others, and what true greatness really looks like in the Kingdom of God. Jesus is teaching some profound and deep spiritual lessons not just for Peter and the other disciples, but for us as well.

We'll never know exactly what it was like on this night together with Jesus in the Upper Room. But because of the adherence to tradition, and the accounts of those who would one day write our Gospels, we can piece together with great confidence many things about that evening, and all the significance it holds.

Rabbis taught that Passover must be observed at a reclining table to symbolize being a Free People, keeping in custom with the traditional Passover custom. Matthew's Gospel describes the scene at the Last Supper beginning this way—

> [20]When evening came, Jesus was reclining at the table with the Twelve. [21]And while they were eating, he said, "Truly I tell you, one of you will betray me." [22]They were very sad and began to say to him one after the other, "Surely you don't mean me, Lord?" (Matthew 26:20-22 NIV)

John, Chapter 13 gives us these details and these words of Jesus.

> [18]"He who shared my bread has turned against me.' [19]"I am telling you now before it happens, so that when it does happen you will believe that I am who I am. [20]Very truly I tell you, whoever accepts anyone I send accepts me; and whoever accepts me accepts the one who sent me." [21]After he had said this, Jesus was troubled in spirit and testified, "Very truly I tell you, one of you is going to betray me." [22]His disciples stared at one another, at a loss to know which of them he meant. [23]One of them, the disciple whom Jesus loved, was reclining next to him. Simon Peter motioned to this disciple and said, "Ask him which one he means." [25]Leaning back against Jesus, he asked him, "Lord, who is it?" [26]Jesus answered, "It is the one to whom I will give this piece of bread when I have dipped it in the dish." Then, dipping the piece of bread, he gave it to Judas, the son of Simon Iscariot.

Biblical historians have suggested that the places in which the disciples are sitting during the Passover meal that night have great significance. John is next to Jesus, close enough to ask a question and possibly on his right. In Jewish culture, this often suggests a place of honor. Judas, it seems, is sitting at his left, in a seat called, "the place of the intimate friend."[2] Jesus places Judas close enough that he dips with Him in the bowl, and close enough to confirm to Judas that he is the betrayer.

On this side of heaven, we'll never know the intricacies of that evening or the fullness of the thoughts behind the words and actions of Jesus. Throughout His ministry, Jesus had often asked Peter and John alone to accompany Him on occasions where the rest of the twelve were not present. And both Peter and John had been asked to prepare this very Passover meal for Jesus and the rest of the disciples. But while John is seated to the right of Jesus in the place of honor, we can't tell where Peter is seated that night.

Could it be that Jesus, in an act of all-knowing sovereignty and unexplainable grace, gives Judas, the man He knew would later betray Him, the other place of honor? He already knows that Judas must carry through with his betrayal so that prophecy could be fulfilled. Yet instead of acting harshly toward him, Jesus, in a stunning act of humility, grace, and power, keeps Judas close, in the place reserved for an intimate friend.

Peter, who was often considered the leader of the disciples, undoubtedly had known what it was like to sit in that place of honor close to Jesus, but on this night, Jesus is using that place to send a message. We can't tell from the text if Peter is too far from Jesus to ask Him a question directly, or if he is just uncharacteristically nervous or too reserved to ask Jesus himself. All we know is that Peter motions *to John*, for *him* to ask Jesus who the betrayer is.

Is it possible that Jesus is not just sending a message to Judas, but to Peter, too? Jesus continues to model what it looks like to lead with both authority and humility and to serve those you are in a position to lead. We've already noted how, on this night, Jesus does not assume a seat at the table waiting to be served, but instead, is actually the most active one at the table, taking on the role that would usually be performed by a servant.

There is great intention behind the words and actions of Jesus here. He tells them they are not to be like those that lord their authority over others, speaking these words—

> **26But you are not to be like that. Instead, the greatest among you should be like the youngest, and the one who rules like the one who serves. 27For who is greater, the one who is at the table or the one who serves? Is it not the one who is at the table? But I am among you as one who serves. (Luke 22: 26-27 NIV)**

Jesus is giving them a clear vision of servant leadership. It *does* feel unnatural to see the greatest among them take on the form of a servant, but *isn't that always the way of Jesus?* He is painting a picture of His gospel right before them with a moment they'll not soon forget.

Maybe Jesus wants Peter to know what it's like to serve, not only those he will lead, but also those who will persecute him, as well. The way He positions Judas that night models that posture. Judas would betray Jesus, and in doing so, each of the disciples as well. But Jesus loves him to the end. He shows the disciples what it looks like to love those who may be hard to love and to lead from a posture of serving.

When Peter made his confession of faith, Jesus spoke of how He would build His Church. Those days will be in a chapter of the story that is still far off and yet to come. But Jesus is using this last night together to give Peter and the other disciples eyes to see what it means to lead in the Kingdom of Christ. The entire New Testament Church would begin with the people in this room, and more than anything, He wants them to get this—*to lead is to take on the posture of serving and loving those you lead.*

On this night, it is Jesus who will be betrayed. But in the days to come, the Church as a whole will be persecuted. Each of the remaining eleven disciples will one day see suffering and persecution. Followers will fall away. Jesus is showing them how to lead with authority from a posture of humility. And in doing so, He is teaching them their role as followers of Jesus, both individually and as a Church. Not to be served, but to serve.

Jesus lives out before them what it is to be the one to hold the position of authority *and* to take on the posture of a servant. And for Peter and the others, they see before them, that, in the Kingdom of God, *it is less about where you are positioned*, and more about *your willingness to serve there, wherever you are.*

GRAINFIELDS, ISRAEL

21

³¹"Simon, Simon, behold, Satan has demanded permission to sift you like wheat; ³²but I have prayed for you, that your faith may not fail; and you, when once you have turned again, strengthen your brothers." ³³But he said to Him, "Lord, with You I am ready to go both to prison and to death!" ³⁴And He said, "I say to you, Peter, the rooster will not crow today until you have denied three times that you know Me."

Luke 22:31-34 (NASB)

What does it mean to be "sifted like wheat?" If you are unfamiliar with the process, it would be easy to miss the significance of the word picture here. The "sifting of wheat," was a process in which, after the wheat was picked, it was shaken back and forth in a sieve until the waste separated itself from the part of the grain to be used.[1] With that in mind, the word picture Jesus uses here describes a process that would shake the faith of His disciples, breaking it down in an attempt to show if it would fail or falter.

There are actually some meaningful lessons hidden within this moment. The original Greek word used, *eksaitéomai*, describes how Satan "asked" for a full "handing over." This would speak to the enemy's attempt to make the disciples' faith fail.[2] It's also interesting that the word "you" in verse 31 is plural, referring to *all the disciples*. But in verse 32, the "you" is singular, meaning *only Peter*.[3] This is obvious in the Greek translation, but it can be easy to miss the fullness of what Jesus is saying here in some English translations. Jesus is telling Peter that *all* the disciples' faith will be tested.

In this moment, Jesus is speaking to Peter, warning him that the enemy wants to test the faith of all the disciples in a way that would tempt them to step away from their faith altogether. The original Greek words used here bring clarity and specify the detail that Jesus then speaks directly to Peter alone, saying, "*But I have prayed for you, Peter, that you would stay faithful to me no matter what comes.*"

Jesus is trying to prepare their hearts for what is to come. He wants them to know that *all* of the disciples will be tempted and tested. They are about to enter a fire that will either burn them up entirely or refine them like gold.

But when Jesus speaks directly to Peter, it's as if He's saying, "Peter, I already know that you will be tested, but I've already been praying for you when that moment comes." The verb described here is actually used in the past tense, meaning, Jesus has already known the moment is coming and has already, *in the past tense,* been praying for Peter in the moment when he will be tested.[4] Not only is Jesus not surprised or disappointed that this moment is even possible, He knows it is coming and has already gone before Peter in it. How incredible that Jesus Christ and God the Father do not stand back and watch to see if Peter, or the disciples, or any of us, will have the strength to endure in faith. Jesus speaks of His own prayers for Peter, asking God to do what needs to be done in order to preserve Peter's faith in that moment of temptation and testing.

The very heart of Jesus is wrapped up in the way that He responds next. Jesus has already prayed to the Father and believes He will answer, when He says, "*And when you have turned again, strengthen your brothers.*" Jesus already knows that Peter will deny Him three times, but He doesn't seem to view this denial as a victory for the enemy or a permanent change of course for Peter. Jesus seems to speak with an assuredness that Peter will deny Him, but then with the same assuredness, He also speaks of Peter turning back to Him.

Peter's faith will be tested, but it will not be abandoned. The prayers that *Jesus has already been praying* will go on to strengthen Peter, drawing him back to Jesus again. Peter will not be left without a shield to fight the temptations of the enemy. Jesus has already gone before him, making a way back to Himself in restoration before the testing of his faith even begins. Jesus has already told us this about Himself in John 10:27-28.

> [27]My sheep hear my voice, I know them, and they follow me. [28]I give them eternal life, and they will never perish. No one will snatch them out of my hand.

Jesus is already aware of the ways that we will face temptations and testing. He may give permission for us to endure things that will refine us, but make no mistake—*He will not allow us to be snatched from His hand.* The hands of the Father and the Son are wrapped fully around us, even as we walk through the flames of the refining fire. And though we may be knocked down and shaken to our very core, we will not fall through the sieve. His loving hand will hold us fast. The words of Jesus are true of our own souls, just as it was for Peter that night, just hours before Peter would do the one thing he so confidently insisted he never would.

Jesus predicts that each of the disciples would be tempted, tested, and sifted like wheat. Yet He prays specific prayers for Peter's faith to be strengthened. In doing so, Jesus is actually providing strength and care for *all* of His brothers. His heart is already set on their restoration. Long before the events of this fateful night unfold, Jesus knew each one of them. He had already gone before the Father in prayer for these men that He loves. And here, He is giving Peter the plan for what to do when it happens.

He already sees. He already knows. And there is such kindness in the way that Jesus anticipates the struggle in the soul of Peter. There is such love in the way He is already pastoring Peter's heart through the moment that is to come.

Peter, perhaps bolstered by his own pride, does not yet know the fullness of the ways his own commitment to Jesus will never be enough. Like a soldier bravely charging into battle, Peter boldly proclaims that he is ready to go to prison or even to death for Jesus. And we believe that *he believes* that. Peter responds to Jesus from a place of his own commitment, but Jesus is already speaking His Covenant over Peter, and the rest of his brothers.

Peter is not alone in his desire to rise to the occasion when it matters most. We can all identify with the hope that we would zealously stand with Jesus with unshakeable faith. The life-changing paradigm shift here is that Jesus is already setting the stage for one of the great wonders of the gospel—that our relationship is not based on how well our faith in Him performs.

Jesus already knows that in this broken world, we will endure suffering. Our faith will be tested, and we will all fall short. But we have a Savior whose love stretches across the great cavern of our failings and across the sea of our shifting faith. Jesus leaves a breadcrumb trail again back to His heart, ever beating the great gospel message of grace—*"My Covenant is greater than your commitment."*

And on this night, Jesus already knows that each of the disciples will falter and fall away. Yet still, He is already speaking His Covenant over them, talking about their future at His table in the Kingdom.

This interaction between Jesus, Peter, and the other disciples is the perfect picture of His Covenant. Our faith is not simply about our hands reaching to the Father but, even more so, about His hands reaching to us. It is not just that our eyes are on God but that His eyes are on us. It is not just our prayers to Jesus, but His prayers for us. The prayers of Jesus sustain our faith. It is not our commitment to Him, but His Covenant with us that holds us. It is less about our own faith or our own abilities, and more about His perfect love toward us. Jesus already sees beyond the present testing of our faith and is already holding us up.

He is already speaking Covenant over the inadequacy of our commitment. And in His Covenant, there is a hope that goes beyond human understanding. There is a sigh of relief.

There is a call to holiness but also a covering of holiness. The greatest gift is *His presence with us* in our joy and in our suffering. And on this sacred night, Peter is still very much in the middle of the story. He can't see it clearly yet, but one day, he'll see with eyes that have been opened. We'll see our own selves in Peter, and we'll remember when the sureness of his commitment walked into the fire and came out refined by the Covenant Love of Jesus.

One day in the distant future, and much later in Scripture, Peter himself will speak these words to us, and we'll remember his time of testing, and hear the heart of Jesus imprinted in his words.

> [12] **Dear friends, do not be surprised at the fiery ordeal that has come on you to test you, as though something strange were happening to you.** [13] **But rejoice inasmuch as you participate in the sufferings of Christ, so that you may be overjoyed when his glory is revealed." (I Peter 4:12-13 NIV)**

KIDRON VALLEY TOWARD THE MOUNT OF OLIVES

22

When they had sung the hymn, they went out to the Mount of Olives.

Matthew 26:30 (ESV)

Have you ever wondered what hymn Jesus and the disciples sing as they leave the Upper Room and go to the Mount of Olives? An essential part of the Passover ritual is the singing of *the Hallel*. The word *Hallel* means *"Praise God!"* And the *Hallel* consists of Psalms 113-118, which are all Psalms of Praise.[1] The Hebrew translation of Matthew 26:30 uses the word "hymn" as translated from the Hebrew word, *Hallel*.[2] It is where the word *hallelujah* comes from, which literally means "praise Yahweh."[3]

It is widely suggested that the song that Jesus, Peter, and the disciples sing just before the departure for the Mount of Olives includes Psalms 115-118, the portion of the songs of praise designated for after the meal.[4] Once again, it is noteworthy that for Jesus and Peter and the other disciples, singing these hymns would have been a part of their Passover experiences year after year, their whole lives. The words of these hymns profoundly point to the Messiah, so it must have been especially poignant for Jesus and the disciples to sing them together that night—especially as Jesus knows what is to come.

Interestingly, Peter and the disciples would have called Jesus either "Rabbi" or by his given Hebrew name for "Jesus", which is *Yeshua*. It is the name that the angel gives in Matthew 1:21 which says "you shall call His name Jesus (*Yeshua*) for it is He who will save His people from their sin." It is not quite as obvious in English, or even the Greek translation, but the name "Jesus" is the transliteration of the Hebrew term, for "the LORD is salvation."[5]

The word "salvation" appears in the Hallel, specifically in Psalm 116:13, Psalm 118:14, and Psalm 118:21. In the original Hebrew, the word for "salvation"—*yeshuah*—is used. *Yeshuah* is literally defined as "salvation."[6] The incredibly poignant connection is that it's possible that when Jesus and the disciples sing the Hallel, they would have been singing, *"yeshua,"* as the word for *salvation. Yeshua is the Jewish way to say "Jesus." And Yeshua is the way to salvation for all people.*[7]

After their sacred evening together, Jesus and Peter and the other disciples sing the Hallel… these hymns that are all about *yeshuah,* God's Salvation, sent for His people. And as Jesus sings these words, He would literally begin His journey into the Garden, willingly stepping into His great sacrifice on the Cross which would *accomplish salvation*, once and for all. The offering of His body and His blood will soon bring forth that salvation…and *Yeshua will truly become the very nature of His name… salvation for us all.*

Singing the name *Yeshua, about Jesus and with Jesus* that evening must have marked Peter deeply. Peter himself would later to go on to say,

> "There is salvation in no one else, for there is no other name under heaven given
> to people by which we must be saved." (Acts 4:12 CSB)

The familiar passage in Philippians 2:9-11 echoes that we find salvation *in the name of Jesus*, the name above all names.

> [9]God highly exalted Him, and bestowed on Him the name which is above every
> name, [10]so that at the name of Jesus every knee will bow, of those who are in
> heaven and on earth and under the earth, [11]and that every tongue will confess
> that Jesus Christ is Lord, to the glory of God the Father.

In your own Bible, read through Psalms 113-118—the familiar Psalms that make up the Hallel. And look closely at these passages in Psalm 116 and 118 that speak about *salvation, yeshuah* in Hebrew. Imagine Peter and the other disciples singing them together with Jesus Himself, as they leave the Upper Room and make their way to the Garden to begin the road to the Cross.

> [4] Then I called on the name of the Lord: "Lord, save me!"
> [5] The Lord is gracious and righteous; our God is compassionate.
> [6] The Lord guards the inexperienced; I was helpless, and he saved me.
> [7] Return to your rest, my soul, for the Lord has been good to you.

⁸ For you, Lord, rescued me from death, my eyes from tears, my feet from stumbling.

⁹ I will walk before the Lord in the land of the living.

¹⁰ I believed, even when I said, "I am severely oppressed."

¹¹ In my alarm I said, "Everyone is a liar."

¹² How can I repay the Lord for all the good he has done for me?

¹³ I will take the cup of salvation (*yeshuah*) and call on the name of the Lord.

(Psalm 116:4-13 CSB)

¹⁴ The Lord is my strength and my song; he has become my salvation. *(yeshuah)*

¹⁵ There are shouts of joy and victory in the tents of the righteous: "The Lord's right hand performs valiantly!

¹⁶ The Lord's right hand is raised. The Lord's right hand performs valiantly!"

¹⁷ I will not die, but I will live and proclaim what the Lord has done.

(Psalm 118:14-17 CSB)

¹⁹ Open the gates of righteousness for me; I will enter through them and give thanks to the Lord.

²⁰ This is the Lord's gate; the righteous will enter through it.

²¹ I will give thanks to you because you have answered me and have become my salvation (*yeshuah*).

²² The stone that the builders rejected has become the cornerstone.

²³ This came from the Lord; it is wondrous in our sight.

²⁴ This is the day the Lord has made; let us rejoice and be glad in it.

²⁵ Lord, save us! Lord, please grant us success!

²⁶ He who comes in the name of the Lord is blessed. From the house of the Lord we bless you.

²⁷ The Lord is God and has given us light. Bind the festival sacrifice with cords to the horns of the altar.

²⁸ You are my God, and I will give you thanks. You are my God; I will exalt you.

²⁹ Give thanks to the Lord, for he is good; his faithful love endures forever.

(Psalm 118:19-29 CSB)

KIDRON VALLEY TOWARD THE MOUNT OF OLIVES

23

³⁰And when they had sung a hymn, they went out to the Mount of Olives.

³¹Then Jesus said to them, "You will all fall away because of me this night. For it is written, 'I will strike the shepherd, and the sheep of the flock will be scattered.' ³²But after I am raised up, I will go before you to Galilee."

Matthew 26: 30-32 (ESV)

The great significance for us is that Jesus not only walks onto the Mount of Olives, but He also willingly steps into the events that He knows must happen. Here, we see once again how Jesus tries to prepare the hearts of His disciples for all that is to come. Despite the frankness of His Words, we get the impression that the fullness of what is about to happen is still lost on them.

Jesus already knows how this night will play out. It will not be a surprise when the commitment of these dear brothers will fall short. He tells them plainly, "you will *all* fall away because of me this night."

He references the passage in Zechariah 13 that prophesies how the shepherd will be struck down and the sheep will be scattered. But there is another layer here to what Jesus is saying, as He prepares the hearts of His disciples.

In many countries, a shepherd drives their flock from behind them, pushing them forward. But an Eastern shepherd interestingly always leads from the front. He walks before the sheep, preparing the way for them.[1] *This is Jesus.* He is their Good Shepherd in every way. He knows that the time will very soon come when He will surrender Himself over to begin the process of suffering to the point of death—to bring redemption to the world.

And like the Good Shepherd that He is, *He walks ahead of them, preparing their hearts for what is to come.*

We can only wonder if it even begins to sink in when He tells them, "You will all fall away because of me this night." Jesus is not only preparing their hearts for what is going to happen, but in His graciousness, He is already pastoring their hearts through what will become their own period of pain and suffering.

The intentional way of Jesus and His thoughtfulness to anticipate the heart-wrenching suffering of His brothers is so meaningful. In verse 32, Jesus leaves a breadcrumb that is so subtle, it's almost easy to miss. Jesus tells Peter and the disciples exactly what will happen after they've all fallen away.

"But after I am raised up, I will go before you to Galilee."

Once again, we can only wonder if they are comprehending the weight in these powerful words from Jesus. First, Jesus confirms that *He will be raised up.* They'd seen Him bring Jairus' daughter and Lazarus back to life. And they'd heard Jesus Himself preach over and over that the Messiah would be killed and rise up again on the third day. But did their minds ever comprehend that His Words were *literal?* The subtle hint and the breadcrumb trail pave the way for what will be up ahead, long after the dark night of the Crucifixion.

"But after I am raised up, I will go before you to Galilee."

They certainly could have missed it on the front side of all that is about to unfold. It's almost as if Jesus is reading them the director's notes from a script. He is going through the motions with them before they actually take place. It's as if He is telling them, "it's going to feel dangerous, and scary, and confusing, but I am choosing to step into what is required for redemption to be set in motion. I will offer myself over. I will be arrested, beaten, pressed, and crushed. Because of Me and what they will do to Me, you will all fall away. I will be put to death, *but three days later I will rise again. And I'll be waiting for you on the other side.*

After the betrayal, and denial, and mourning, and death, *I will be waiting for you in Galilee.*" It would have been especially important to Jesus that Peter hear Him say those words, even if all they are now is a deposit into what will become Peter's memory long after this dark night. Jesus wants Peter and the others to hear Him say these words so that in their darkest hours, the light of His words would lead the way back to Him. "I will go before you, and I will meet you there on the other side." In the words of Psalm 30:5,

"Weeping may last for the night, But a shout of joy comes in the morning."

The posture of Jesus toward His disciples here is a perfect display of His Covenant being greater than their commitment. He knows that the events that are about to unfold will break them. And even the most loyal, brave, and pure-hearted among them could still never *commit* their way through this.

There is a cavern between what their *commitment* could accomplish and what only His *Covenant* can fulfill. There will be grave danger and paralyzing fear. They will see things that will break their spirits, and they will feel things that will break their hearts. Jesus already knows they will all fall away. In fact, it has always been foretold this way. They'd heard the words of Zechariah their whole lives. How were they to know that *they were the sheep that would scatter* and it is actually *their Good Shepherd* who will be struck down?

But Jesus knows. And He is already going before them. He wants them to have His words ringing in their ears and imprinted deep in their hearts when they find themselves alone and afraid. He knows, like sheep they will scatter, but He is already shepherding them back to Himself. And it is His Covenant that will be the road back to Him.

He will go before them.
And He'll be waiting for them there,
in Galilee…
Back on the familiar shores of where it all began…
Back where He'd called them, and taught them, and changed their lives forever.

THE MOUNT OF OLIVES

24

³³Peter told him, "Even if everyone falls away because of you, I will never fall away."

³⁴"Truly I tell you," Jesus said to him, "tonight, before the rooster crows, you will deny me three times."

³⁵"Even if I have to die with you," Peter told him, "I will never deny you," and all the disciples said the same thing.

Matthew 26:33-35 (CSB)

If there's one thing we know about Peter by now, it's that he pretty consistently speaks boldly and quickly. In this moment, we might even be able to believe, that *he believes* it's true as he promises that he'll never fall away. Peter is the very picture of commitment. He drops his nets and follows Jesus, he jumps out of the water to walk to Jesus, and here, he promises that his commitment will stand firm *even if everyone else falls away*. But even still, these are the words of Jesus to Peter on this night—

"Truly I tell you, tonight, before the rooster crows, you will deny me three times."

Jesus and Peter have been in a moment like this before. This is not the first time they are at a crossroads where Jesus says something will happen, and Peter protests. In the past, when Peter hasn't been able to wrap his mind around something, he has been quick to speak up. He's even been the guy that *rebukes Jesus* when he feels like there might be a better way. But this time, it has to feel personal. Jesus is suggesting that *Peter* will deny Him. And Peter can't fathom it.

It can be said that Peter has a history of being impulsive or bold, but it should also be said that he has a history of being brave—of stepping out in faith, even when everyone around him remains still. Peter may have followed Jesus imperfectly, and he may have spoken foolishly on occasion, but his commitment to Jesus would have never been in question. Perhaps that's why this interaction with Jesus feels so personal to him. John's Gospel, in chapter 13, gives us another glimpse and a deeper insight into their interaction that night.

> [33] **"My children, I will be with you only a little longer. You will look for me, and just as I told the Jews, so I tell you now: Where I am going, you cannot come.** [34] **A new command I give you: Love one another. As I have loved you, so you must love one another.** [35] **By this everyone will know that you are my disciples, if you love one another."** [36] **Simon Peter asked him, "Lord, where are you going?"**
>
> **Jesus replied, "Where I am going, you cannot follow now, but you will follow later."** [37] **Peter asked, "Lord, why can't I follow you now? I will lay down my life for you."** [38] **Then Jesus answered, "Will you really lay down your life for me? Very truly I tell you, before the rooster crows, you will disown me three times!"**

Peter has always been comfortable enough with Jesus to ask hard questions. But Peter has also been close enough to be truly humbled by the sheer majesty of Jesus. Who's to say how any of us would have acted in the actual presence of Jesus?

We can empathize with Peter here. After three years of giving his life to following Jesus, it isn't as if his commitment has been complacent. He's dropped everything to follow Jesus. He changed his entire life to sit under this Rabbi's teaching and to follow Him as a disciple. It's easy to understand that part inside of Peter that rises up and wants to prove somehow that his heart really is *for Jesus*, and that he has no intention of ever leaving. When Jesus had said, "Come, Follow Me," Peter had followed, and his heart is to *keep following Jesus*, wherever that may lead.

What Peter doesn't understand, of course, is all that is about to unfold. Jesus has tried to prepare his heart, but who would have anticipated that God's plan was to allow for things to unfold the way they will?

You can almost hear it in his voice when he protests back to Jesus—"even if I have to *die with you, I will never deny you."*

Peter's commitment to Jesus is great, but Jesus knows what is coming against him will be great, as well. Ultimately, what matters most is that the *Covenant love of Jesus is greater than all of it.*

In fact, as Jesus is telling them He must go away, John 13 shows us that He gives them this command–

"Love one another. As I have loved you, so you must love one another. By this

everyone will know that you are my disciples if you love one another."

Jesus is preparing them. As He knows the time has come to go away, He begins the conversation about the way that He loves them. Then, He encourages them to love in that same way. But in Peter's mind, that conversation will have to wait.

Peter isn't thinking about love. He is stuck back on the first thing Jesus had said. *All Peter hears is that Jesus is going somewhere.* And one thing that continues to be true of Peter is his desire to be near Jesus. On a boat, out of the boat, on the water, up the mountain—Jesus had asked him to follow, and Peter has been following closely ever since. He has no intention of backing off now.

But Jesus says that Peter will deny Him three times that very night. In fact, *all* of the disciples will fall away. And not just the disciples, not just that night in the garden, but *each of us, over and over again.*

Every single one of us—even the boldest followers among us—will at times deny Him, or fall asleep, or fall away in our own ways. Even our greatest commitment to Him is not enough.

But still, His Covenant is greater. It is not dependent on our ability to answer the questions with courage, to do the right thing, or to even keep our commitment in faith. Jesus knows that in our human brokenness, we simply cannot do it on our own. So, He made a way. He took on our shame and our sin to be with us. The apostle Paul reminds us,

> "God shows his love for us in that while we were still sinners, Christ died for us."
> (Romans 5:8 ESV)

And when our completely inadequate, imperfect commitment fails or falters, His great Covenant love stretches to the places where our commitment runs out. He meets us there, just as we are.

His Covenant is greater than our commitment.

THE MOUNT OF OLIVES

25

¹"Do not let your hearts be troubled. You believe in God; believe also in me. ² My Father's house has many rooms; if that were not so, would I have told you that I am going there to prepare a place for you? ³ And if I go and prepare a place for you, I will come back and take you to be with me that you also may be where I am. ⁴ You know the way to the place where I am going."

¹⁵ "If you love me, keep my commands. ¹⁶ And I will ask the Father, and he will give you another advocate to help you and be with you forever— ¹⁷ the Spirit of truth. The world cannot accept him, because it neither sees him nor knows him. But you know him, for he lives with you and will be in you. ¹⁸ I will not leave you as orphans; I will come to you. ¹⁹ Before long, the world will not see me anymore, but you will see me. Because I live, you also will live. ²⁰ On that day you will realize that I am in my Father, and you are in me, and I am in you. ²¹ Whoever has my commands and keeps them is the one who loves me. The one who loves me will be loved by my Father, and I too will love them and show myself to them."

²⁵ "All this I have spoken while still with you. ²⁶ But the Advocate, the Holy Spirit, whom the Father will send in my name, will teach you all things and will remind you of everything I have said to you. ²⁷ Peace I leave with you; my peace I give you. I do not give to you as the world gives. Do not let your hearts be troubled and do not be afraid.

²⁸ You heard me say, 'I am going away and I am coming back to you.' If you loved me, you would be glad that I am going to the Father, for the Father is greater than I. ²⁹ I have told you now before it happens, so that when it does happen you will believe. ³⁰ I will not say much more to you, for the prince of this world is coming. He has no hold over me, ³¹ but he comes so that the world may learn that I love the Father and do exactly what my Father has commanded me.
Come now; let us leave."

John 14:1-4, 15-21, 25-31 (NIV)

Have you ever wondered what it would be like to know when your time on earth is running out? What would be going through your mind? What would you want your final conversations to be about? It would be understandable to want to speak as many words of life and love over your friends and family in those last moments. It would be natural to hope that you'd imparted wisdom and made impressions into those you love that will last long after you're gone. It's sometimes said that at the end of life, there often comes a newfound sense of clarity for what really matters most in life. That perspective has a way of distilling down the types of things that matter to a very short list.

As we read in this passage here, as Jesus gathers with His disciples knowing that His time with them on earth is coming to an end. He's spent three years with them, preaching, teaching and pouring into them. But now, Jesus wants to bring peace to their souls in these last moments. Peace not as the world gives, but *a peace that He brings with His presence.*

He wants to tell them about the Holy Spirit, the Helper who will teach them and bring to their remembrance all that He'd taught them while they'd been together. He wants them to know that while He'll be gone in person, He'll always be with them in Spirit. And He wants to use this time to share some of His *most important parting words of life.*

If you have one of those Bibles that marks the words of Jesus with red lettering, then you can see that in these moments, the Gospel writers shift away from recalling the events, as outsiders looking in.

Instead, they begin to quote those final, life-giving words of Jesus directly. In the gospel of John, chapters 14,15,16, and 17 are all almost completely *written in red.*

At the end of it all, these are the things Jesus wants His disciples to hear most. These last parting words of Jesus carry the weight of profound holiness. You can sense the urgency in this Rabbi, who knows that the time with His beloved disciples is soon running out. He uses what may be His last hour or two with them to speak words of life over them. There are only so many minutes left on the clock, and Jesus knows this is the time to speak to His disciples, and also through them, *to all who would someday follow Him.*

These words in red—they are the words that Jesus wants us to hear and know.

These are the truths that He wants to take root deep in our hearts and our souls. Imagine Jesus in these final hours, surrounded by His disciples as He shares. Imagine Peter there, and the other disciples there, but *imagine yourself there, too…* looking into the eyes of Jesus speaking these words.

Let's read the passage from John again. Read the words and receive them, knowing they are each chosen carefully from the heart of God, for each of us. See the intentional care of a loving Savior and hear His life-giving words.

> 23 Jesus replied, "Loving me empowers you to obey my word. And my Father will love you so deeply that we will come to you and make you our dwelling place.

> 24 But those who don't love me will not obey my words. The Father did not send me to speak my own revelation, but the words of my Father. 25 I am telling you this while I am still with you.

> 26 But when the Father sends the Spirit of Holiness, the One like me who sets you free, he will teach you all things in my name. And he will inspire you to remember every word that I've told you.

> 27 I leave the gift of peace with you—my peace. Not the kind of fragile peace given by the world, but my perfect peace.

> Don't yield to fear or be troubled in your hearts—instead, be courageous!

> 28 Remember what I've told you, that I must go away, but I promise to come back to you. So if you truly love me, you will be glad for me, since I'm returning

to my Father, who is greater than I.

²⁹ So when all of these things happen, you will still trust and cling to me. ³⁰ I won't speak with you much longer, for the ruler of this dark world is coming. But he has no power over me, for he has nothing to use against me. ³¹ I am doing exactly what the Father destined for me to accomplish, so that the world will discover how much I love my Father. Now come with me." (John 14: 23-31 TPT)

VINES IN ISRAEL

26

[1]"I am the true vine, and My Father is the vinedresser. [2] Every branch in Me that does not bear fruit, He takes away; and every branch that bears fruit, He prunes it so that it may bear more fruit. [3] You are already clean because of the word which I have spoken to you. [4] Abide in Me, and I in you. As the branch cannot bear fruit of itself unless it abides in the vine, so neither can you unless you abide in Me. [5] I am the vine, you are the branches; he who abides in Me and I in him, he bears much fruit, for apart from Me you can do nothing. [6] If anyone does not abide in Me, he is thrown away as a branch and dries up; and they gather them, and cast them into the fire and they are burned. [7] If you abide in Me, and My words abide in you, ask whatever you wish, and it will be done for you. [8] My Father is glorified by this, that you bear much fruit, and so prove to be My disciples. [9] Just as the Father has loved Me, I have also loved you; abide in My love. [10] If you keep My commandments, you will abide in My love; just as I have kept My Father's commandments and abide in His love. [11] These things I have spoken to you so that My joy may be in you, and that your joy may be made full.

[12] This is My commandment, that you love one another, just as I have loved you. [13] Greater love has no one than this, that one lay down his life for his friends. [14] You are My friends if you do what I command you. [15] No longer do I call you slaves, for the slave does not know what his master is doing; but I have called you friends, for all things that I have heard from My Father I have made known to you. [16] You did not choose Me but I chose you, and appointed you that you would go and bear fruit, and that your fruit would remain, so that whatever you ask of the Father in My name He may give to you. [17] This I command you, that you love one another."

John 15: 1-17 (NASB)

During His time with Peter and the other disciples, Jesus shares His seven "I AM" statements. These statements bring truth and clarity to exactly who Jesus is. He's already told them this about Himself…

"I am the Bread of Life."

"I am the Light of the World."

"I am the Gate."

"I am the Good Shepherd."

"I am the Resurrection and the Life."

"I am the Way and the Truth and the Life."

And in these final hours with His brothers, He shares one more "I AM" statement—one more picture He wants to give them of who He really is and who they are *in Him.*

We don't have exact details about exactly where they are in their evening together when Jesus begins sharing this incredibly powerful imagery. Some commentators speculate that they possibly could have been walking alongside vines in a vineyard as they journeyed together, or they may still have been gathered after their meal with views of vines nearby. Regardless of where they are, the disciples are well familiar with the image of vines, branches, and vineyards. Jesus comes around this incredibly life-giving spiritual truth by using something that they can visualize, understand, and possibly even physically see with their own eyes, as He teaches.

John 15 gives us one of the most iconic and spiritually significant pieces of wisdom that Jesus imparts. Jesus uses the familiar imagery of a vine, the vine-dresser, fruit, and branches to help us understand Himself and the New Covenant He's just begun with His people. Jesus says to them in John 15:1, "I am the true vine."

The word picture Jesus is using here might not evoke the same meaning for us today as it would have for a Jewish follower in the first century. Throughout the Old Testament, the imagery of the vine is used to symbolize Israel or God's people. Jesus begins to speak into the lineage and family tree of the people of God who have been unfruitful as they've lived lives striving to keep the law, yet always falling short. Jesus has come to do what they could not do. He has come to fulfill what they could never be without Him. Jesus is using that picture and showing the people of God what it looks like to live *from Him, by abiding in Him* and bearing fruit because of *His life in them.*

Andrew Murray uses these incredible words to speak about Jesus using this imagery. "All earthly things are the shadows of heavenly realities—the expression, in created, visible forms, of the invisible glory of God. The Life and the Truth are in Heaven; on earth we have figures and shadows of the heavenly truths. When Jesus says: 'I am the true Vine,' He tells us that all the vines of earth are pictures and emblems of Himself. He is the divine reality, of which they are the created expression. They all point to Him, and preach Him, and reveal Him."[1]

Let's look at John 15 again. Jesus uses the imagery of the vine and the vine-dresser to help us understand His own relationship with the Father, and how the faith of followers of Jesus flows *from Him, the true Vine.*

> [1]"I am the true vine, and My Father is the vinedresser. [2]Every branch in Me that does not bear fruit, He takes away; and every branch that bears fruit, He prunes it so that it may bear more fruit. [3]You are already clean because of the word which I have spoken to you. [4]Abide in Me, and I in you. As the branch cannot bear fruit of itself unless it abides in the vine, so neither can you unless you abide in Me. [5]I am the vine, you are the branches; he who abides in Me and I in him, he bears much fruit, for apart from Me you can do nothing."

In these sacred last hours, Jesus is trying to give the disciples a clear picture of what it will be like for them as they live in the New Covenant. Jesus will no longer be with them physically, but instead empowering them by the work of the Holy Spirit and what will be His finished work on the cross. Jesus knows their commitment to Him will fail. He knows they will fall. He already knows that just like Israel, they are unable to live out their calling on their own. But He is giving them a visual picture of *literally* what it would look like to begin to live a life apart from striving, apart from meaningless attempts at righteousness before men, and apart from an inability to keep the law. Jesus is instead, giving the invitation to instead live with the power of His finished work pulsing through them as they live out their faith.

Jesus takes these moments to help them begin to understand what it will look like to live a life abiding in Christ. The visual image gives weight to our understanding that Jesus is the vine, and God, the Father, is the one that tends and cares for the vine. All of the followers of Jesus, then, and forever more, are branches *that stem from the life of the vine.* The branches are given life, and nourishment, and grow *because of the vine they are living from.* And for the believer, life on the vine means *pruning, abiding, and bearing fruit.* This is where the action of "abiding" becomes more clear.

The word that Jesus uses here for the word abide is *menó* in Greek, which means "to stay, to abide, to remain, to wait."[2] Our very identity as a branch connected to the vine is given life and power when we choose to live, remain, and *abide in Him.* Our purpose as the branch is to bring forth fruit, but not by our own striving. Here is where the brilliance of the imagery that Jesus uses is so helpful. A branch that has been cut off or fallen from a vine would obviously not continue to bear fruit. It is the very nature of *staying connected to the vine* that gives a branch the ability to bloom, grow, and bear fruit. It is His power *in us as we live from Him* that allows us to grow and bear fruit. The fruit of the branch is a natural overflow of life on the vine.

And pruning of the branch is actually loving protection to help a branch remain in the vine. Jesus knows all that is about to happen for Peter and the other disciples in a few short hours. And in His heart to pastor them through a life that will be newly lived out without Him there beside them, He is giving them profound wisdom that speaks to exactly what their hearts will need to hear.

These are words of life. For Peter, for the disciples, and for each of us, for now and forever more.

THE GARDEN OF GETHSEMANE

27

[36] Then Jesus went with his disciples to a place called Gethsemane, and he said to them, "Sit here while I go over there and pray." [37] He took Peter and the two sons of Zebedee along with him, and he began to be sorrowful and troubled. [38] Then he said to them, "My soul is overwhelmed with sorrow to the point of death. Stay here and keep watch with me."

[39] Going a little farther, he fell with his face to the ground and prayed, "My Father, if it is possible, may this cup be taken from me. Yet not as I will, but as you will."

[40] Then he returned to his disciples and found them sleeping. "Couldn't you men keep watch with me for one hour?" he asked Peter. [41] "Watch and pray so that you will not fall into temptation. The spirit is willing, but the flesh is weak."

[42] He went away a second time and prayed, "My Father, if it is not possible for this cup to be taken away unless I drink it, may your will be done."

[43] When he came back, he again found them sleeping, because their eyes were heavy. [44] So he left them and went away once more and prayed the third time, saying the same thing.

[45] Then he returned to the disciples and said to them, "Are you still sleeping and resting? Look, the hour has come, and the Son of Man is delivered into the hands of sinners. [46] Rise! Let us go! Here comes my betrayer!"

Matthew 26:36-46 (NIV)

The hour has come. As Jesus steps into the garden by the olive press that night, He also steps willingly into all that comes along with the olive press in every way. He is giving Himself up to be crushed, pressed, spilled out, even to the point of death.

As Jesus has been imparting His last words of life and wisdom, He has led them to an olive orchard on the Mount of Olives, a place known as the Garden of Gethsemane, which comes from the words meaning "oil press."[1] In that time, heavy stone slabs were lowered onto olives that had already been crushed in an olive crusher. Gradually, the weight of the slab squeezed the olive oil out of the pulp, and the oil ran into a pit. There, the oil was collected in clay jars. The image of Gethsemane on the slope of the Mount of Olives where Jesus went the night before His crucifixion provides a vivid picture of Jesus' suffering. The weight of the sins of the world pressed down upon Him like a heavy slab of rock pressed down on olives in their baskets. Luke 22:44 adds that His sweat was "like drops of blood falling to the ground," and it flowed from Him like olive oil as it was squeezed out and flowed into the pit of an olive press.[2]

The divine nature of Jesus means He carries all-knowing wisdom about what is getting ready to unfold. But Jesus, though fully God, is also fully man. And His humanity causes Him to be "overwhelmed with sorrow to the point of death." This begins what will be the most treacherous hours Jesus will experience on earth.

And Jesus actually knows exactly what will happen. And His human body begins to respond. With all that is stirring in Him, Jesus knows He needs to go to the Father in prayer. In His darkest hours, Jesus asks His closest brothers, Peter, James, and John, to stay and keep watch as He prays.

Jesus says, "My soul is overwhelmed with sorrow to the point of death. Stay here and keep watch with me." He is physically overcome by the full knowledge of what He is about to endure. As the sorrow and angst envelop Him, He offers up one last prayer.

"My Father, if it is possible, may this cup be taken from me. Yet not as I will, but as you will."

Luke 22:44 refers to Jesus' ordeal as "agony," a scene that must have been excruciating to watch. It says, "and being in agony he prayed more earnestly; and *his sweat became like great drops of blood falling down to the ground.*"

There, in the place of crushing, and pressing, Jesus begins to feel the full weight of what must happen. Yet even in His angst and anguish, with His face buried in the ground, Jesus re-focuses His gaze on the Father in prayer, offering, "yet not my will, but Yours be done."

Jesus had asked the three disciples to keep watch as He prayed, but not only did they not keep watch, *they didn't even stay awake.* When He returns and finds them sleeping, *it's Peter* that He questions. "Couldn't you men keep watch with me for one hour?" He asked Peter.

"Watch and pray so that you will not fall into temptation. The spirit is willing, but the flesh is weak."

It's important to note that Jesus speaks only to Peter here. All three of them—Peter, James, and John—had been asked to pray, and *all three* had fallen asleep. But *it's Peter* that Jesus questions and reprimands. Is it because Peter has been particularly vocal and even zealous about what he was willing to do *for Jesus?* The man who'd just said *he would die with Jesus* is now not even able to *stay awake with Him?*

There is a knowing—a foreshadowing almost—in the words Jesus chooses to use here. *"The spirit is willing, but the flesh is weak."*

Does Peter hear it? Does he feel the weight that those words hold? The meaning of the original word Jesus uses here for "flesh" generally relates to "unaided human effort... decisions and actions that originate from self or are empowered by self." This "flesh" proceeds out of the untouched, unchanged part of us—what is not transformed by God.[3]

It's been a meaningful night, with several bold commitments made by Peter already. But the night is far from over, and there will be many opportunities for *"the flesh"* to be tested. This garden isn't the first to hold within it a spirit that is willing, but a flesh that is weak. And the temptation that Jesus speaks of is from a tale as old as time, literally, *garden and all.*

The flesh—that unaided human effort, the part *empowered by self,* not transformed by God—is very often indeed weak, even if the spirit is more willing.

It's only a brief time before Jesus returns and finds them asleep *again. Three times, in fact, they fall asleep.* Luke 22:45 says, "When he got up from prayer and came to the disciples, he found them sleeping, exhausted from their grief." Perhaps there is a deeper meaning attached to the way the disciples keep falling asleep. It is a picture of the frailty of being human. Even if the spirit, *the commitment,* is great, there is always still *"flesh,"* and a limit to that which is humanly possible, apart from God.

But there is also a picture here of how God covers over the gaps of what *"the flesh"* is unable to sustain. Luke, Chapter 22, verses 43-46 is the only Gospel that gives us yet another brushstroke of how the portrait of this night in the garden looks in full.

> **An angel from heaven appeared to him and strengthened him. And being in anguish, he prayed more earnestly, and his sweat was like drops of blood falling to the ground. When he rose from prayer and went back to the disciples, he found them asleep, exhausted from sorrow. "Why are you sleeping?" he asked them. "Get up and pray so that you will not fall into temptation."**

In agony and anguish, Jesus goes to the Father, and the Father, in His great love, sends an angel to strengthen Him. Jesus gives everything over to the Father, and as He prays, He is so fortified that by the time He rises from His prayer, He is resolute in His mission. Knowing what is about to happen does not make Him run or back down. Instead, out of His great love, *Jesus allows it to begin.*

THE GARDEN OF GETHSEMANE

28

² Now Judas, who betrayed him, knew the place, because Jesus had often met there with his disciples. ³ So Judas came to the garden, guiding a detachment of soldiers and some officials from the chief priests and the Pharisees. They were carrying torches, lanterns and weapons.

⁴ Jesus, knowing all that was going to happen to him, went out and asked them, "Who is it you want?" ⁵ "Jesus of Nazareth," they replied.

"I am he," Jesus said. (And Judas the traitor was standing there with them.)

⁶ When Jesus said, "I am he," they drew back and fell to the ground.

⁷ Again he asked them, "Who is it you want?" "Jesus of Nazareth," they said.

⁸ Jesus answered, "I told you that I am he. If you are looking for me, then let these men go." ⁹ This happened so that the words he had spoken would be fulfilled: "I have not lost one of those you gave me."

¹⁰ Then Simon Peter, who had a sword, drew it and struck the high priest's servant, cutting off his right ear. (The servant's name was Malchus.)

¹¹ Jesus commanded Peter, "Put your sword away! Shall I not drink the cup the Father has given me?"

John 18: 2-11 (NIV)

Having been part of the close inner circle, Judas knew right where Jesus would be, and he guides the soldiers right to Him. The original word used here in John 18:3 for the "detachment of soldiers" is actually the Greek word, *speira* meaning "band of men." This is the word that describes a military cohort—a *group of 300 to 600 soldiers, perhaps even up to 1,000 men*.[1] These extremely well-trained soldiers were equipped with the finest weaponry of the day. John 18:3 also tells us that on the night Jesus was arrested, this band of Roman soldiers was accompanied by "officers from the Chief Priests and Pharisees" as well. So the cohort of soldiers, *plus* the Temple Police would have made for a very large crowd, most likely *several hundred men!*[2] John 18:3 even says "they were carrying torches, lanterns and weapons," which most likely indicates that they were anticipating having to search for the man they wanted to arrest. *But Jesus steps up in authority. He doesn't hide, and He doesn't falter.* Jesus had once told them in John 10: 17, 18—

> "I lay down my life so that I may take it up again. No one takes it from me, but
> I lay it down on my own. I have the right to lay it down, and I have the right to
> take it up again. I have received this command from my Father."

In this moment, no one is taking anything from Jesus. *He is allowing this to happen.* He is stepping forward in authority and power. He knows it must happen, and even though it will bring the greatest suffering any human has ever known, He willingly steps forward and into the process by which He will willingly lay down His life.

> [4]Jesus, knowing all that was going to happen to him, went out and asked them,
> "Who is it you want?" [5]"Jesus of Nazareth," they replied. "I am he," Jesus said.
> (And Judas the traitor was standing there with them.) [6]When Jesus said, "I am
> he," they drew back and fell to the ground.

With the sound of His voice, *they draw back and fall to the ground.* The Greek word used here describes an action that is to fall prostrate on one's face, overcome by terror or astonishment or grief.[3] Jesus is not a common thief, hiding in the shadows, and caught in the act. This is the wild and wondrous voice of God, thundering and proclaiming, "*I am He.*" His very words cause them to buckle before Him. And yet, there He stands, firmly in the will of His Father, with authority and power and driven by a relentless love for His people.

> [7]Again he asked them, "Who is it you want?" "Jesus of Nazareth," they said. [8]Je-
> sus answered, "I told you that I am he. If you are looking for me, then let these
> men go." [9]This happened so that the words he had spoken would be fulfilled: "I
> have not lost one of those you gave me." [10]Then Simon Peter, who had a sword,
> drew it and struck the high priest's servant, cutting off his right ear. (The ser-
> vant's name was Malchus.) [11]Jesus commanded Peter, "Put your sword away!
> Shall I not drink the cup the Father has given me?"

Peter cannot imagine letting this happen. He is bolstered by protective instinct, compelled by fierce love and armed, not with a long, powerful sword befitting battle, but rather a short dagger, similar to his fishing knife.[4] His love for Jesus and his desire to keep Him from harm erupt in a flood of emotion, and somebody loses an ear.

This isn't the first time that Peter protests. He's been here before. Sometimes the ways of Jesus don't sit right with him, and Peter always seems to hope there is a better way. Jesus has prepared Peter for this moment. He's told him on more than one occasion what must happen. But Peter isn't willing to go down without a fight…*literally. He is prepared to take on hundreds of men, all on his own, for the cause of Christ.* But Jesus commands Peter to put away his sword.

Much can be said of what Peter is feeling in this moment. But any man who is willing to stand up to a legion of *several hundred men*, all alone, to protect someone he loves—that is a picture of *courageous love.* It may be an imperfect love. It may be the wrong response here. But this is a David and Goliath moment, and even if Peter's zealous commitment is misplaced, it is driven by bold, brave, loyal love.

Peter cannot reconcile in his mind that this is the way it is supposed to happen. But Jesus knows that the journey into these treacherous dark moments—a journey *through death itself*—is the only road that leads to life. He cannot let Peter, even out of fierce love, try to prevent this from coming to pass.

> ⁴⁹When Jesus' followers saw what was going to happen, they said, "Lord, should we strike with our swords?" ⁵⁰And one of them struck the servant of the high priest, cutting off his right ear. ⁵¹But Jesus answered, "No more of this!" And he touched the man's ear and healed him. (Luke 22:49-51 NIV)

The air is thick with the divine, and the miraculous envelopes what happens in "the flesh." Jesus touches the ear of Malchus, reversing what was done at the hands of Peter, bringing restoration and healing in the way that only He can. Not even Peter, with his sword and his emphatic promise, can hold back the hand of Heaven, as the great rescue plan begins. Matthew's Gospel gives even more detail about the words of Jesus in that moment.

> ⁵²Then Jesus told him, "Put your sword back in its place because all who take up the sword will perish by the sword. ⁵³Or do you think that I cannot call on my Father, and he will provide me here and now with more than twelve legions of angels? ⁵⁴How, then, would the Scriptures be fulfilled that say it must happen this way?" ⁵⁵At that time Jesus said to the crowds, "Have you come out with swords and clubs, as if I were a criminal, to capture me? Every day I used to sit, teaching in the temple, and you didn't arrest me. ⁵⁶But all this has happened so that the writings of the prophets would be fulfilled." Then all the disciples deserted him and ran away. (Matthew 26:52-56 CSB)

His Words are a reminder of the truth. If Jesus wanted, He could have called on the Father, and more than twelve legions of angels would have come to His side to free Him from the hands of the enemy. It isn't the power of the arresting guards that holds Jesus there that night. He could have overpowered them in a moment. He *gives* Himself over because it is the way it is supposed to happen. Generations have been watching and waiting to see this prophecy fulfilled. Those with Jesus don't understand it fully. It must have felt confusing and heart-breaking for Peter and the other disciples. But Jesus knows that the cup cannot pass from Him. The long-appointed hour has come. This is the very reason He'd been sent, and *in His great love, Jesus ushers in the beginning of the end.*

HOUSE OF CAIPHAS, THE HIGH PRIEST, JERUSALEM

29

[14]Now Caiaphas was the one who had advised the Jews that it was expedient for one man to die on behalf of the people.

[15]Simon Peter was following Jesus, and so was another disciple. Now that disciple was known to the high priest, and entered with Jesus into the court of the high priest, [16]but Peter was standing at the door outside. So the other disciple, who was known to the high priest, went out and spoke to the doorkeeper, and brought Peter in. [17]Then the slave-girl who kept the door said to Peter, "You are not also one of this man's disciples, are you?" He said, "I am not." [18]Now the slaves and the officers were standing there, having made a charcoal fire, for it was cold and they were warming themselves; and Peter was also with them, standing and warming himself.

[25]Now Simon Peter was standing and warming himself. So they said to him, "You are not also one of His disciples, are you?" He denied it, and said, "I am not." [26]One of the slaves of the high priest, being a relative of the one whose ear Peter cut off, said, "Did I not see you in the garden with Him?" [27]Peter then denied it again, and immediately a rooster crowed.

John 18:14-18, 25-27 (NASB)

Jesus had told Peter this moment would come. Even though it had only been a few hours, it must have felt like a lifetime had passed since they'd all gathered around the table in the Upper Room. The events of the last few hours would change everything. They'd walked with Jesus, and He'd poured out His heart to them. Had they been hanging on every word, with a sense that this was their last night with Him? Or did they listen as they walked and talked, this night feeling no different than all the nights before them?

Judas betrays Jesus with a kiss. But Peter is not about to let things go. Standing before a legion of hundreds of men, *Peter alone* holds up his sword to defend his Savior. Peter is remembered for many things, but he is rarely spoken of as a man of courage. But there, under the moonlight and in the reflection of torches in the garden, his love for Jesus makes him brave.

We don't often hear or think about Peter as the one staying close to Jesus on this night, but he actually follows Him right into the most dangerous place he could be. There is "another disciple" left standing, and while his name is not given, it is widely believed that disciple is John. All the other disciples are nowhere to be found. They'd all fallen away, just as Jesus told them they would.

But Peter follows Jesus right into the lion's den. Or at least, as far as he can. Though officials and officers and guards surround him, Peter tries to stay close to Jesus. Peter is running right *into* the danger, desperate to get as close as he can to Jesus. John 18:12 tells us he'd just watched, as "a company of soldiers, the commander and the Jewish officials arrested Jesus and tied Him up." They'd led Him away like a common criminal to the high priest. While all the other supporters of Jesus had fled, John and Peter follow Jesus closely as His accusers take Him deeper inside the walls toward those who are against Him. Peter is not hiding secretly in the shadows from a hidden spot, nearby.

Peter is trying to get as close as he can to Jesus, no matter how dangerous it is. Mark's Gospel reminds us that Peter is close enough to see and hear as the chief priests and the whole Council look for evidence against Jesus so that they can put Him to death. Peter is close inside the courtyard of where Jesus is being held, as the guards begin to spit at Him, and beat Him and taunt Him. Peter is a part of this scene as it unfolds.

> [64]They all condemned him as worthy of death.
> [65]Then some began to spit at him; they blindfolded him, struck him with their fists, and said, "Prophesy!" And the guards took him and beat him.
> [66]While Peter was below in the courtyard, one of the servant girls of the high priest came by.
> [67]When she saw Peter warming himself, she looked closely at him.
> "You also were with that Nazarene, Jesus," she said.
> [68]But he denied it. "I don't know or understand what you're talking about," he said, and went out into the entryway.
> [69]When the servant girl saw him there, she said again to those standing around, "This fellow is one of them."
> [70]Again he denied it. After a little while, those standing near said to Peter, "Surely you are one of them, for you are a Galilean." (Mark 14: 64-70 NIV)

It's been written that there would have been a distinctive dialect common to those who spoke with a Galilean accent.[1] Matthew 26:73 even notes how those near Peter that night even say to him, "surely you are one of them; your accent gives you away." It is evident to those inside the courtyard that night that Peter isn't from around there. And John 18:26 gives further detail that implicates Peter beyond a shadow of a doubt.

> One of the high priest's servants, a relative of the man whose ear Peter had cut off, said, "Didn't I see you with Him in the garden?"

When we remember *where* Peter is, and *what* he is up against at that moment, we can see more clearly just what it is like on this night. His whole life is about to change, and although Jesus has tried to prepare his heart, nothing about this night unfolds in a way that makes sense to Peter.

Most people remember Peter for what happens next. And it's true, he failed; but he failed in a situation which none of the other disciples even dared to face.[2]

NIGHT IN THE OLD CITY, JERUSALEM

30

⁶⁹Now Peter was sitting out in the courtyard, and a servant girl came to him. "You also were with Jesus of Galilee," she said.

⁷⁰But he denied it before them all. "I don't know what you're talking about," he said.

⁷¹Then he went out to the gateway, where another servant girl saw him and said to the people there, "This fellow was with Jesus of Nazareth."

⁷²He denied it again, with an oath: "I don't know the man!"

⁷³After a little while, those standing there went up to Peter and said, "Surely you are one of them; your accent gives you away."

⁷⁴Then he began to call down curses, and he swore to them, "I don't know the man!"

Immediately a rooster crowed. ⁷⁵Then Peter remembered the word Jesus had spoken: "Before the rooster crows, you will disown me three times." And he went outside and wept bitterly.

Matthew 26: 69-75 (NIV)

Jesus had told him what would happen. He even told Peter what it would sound like when he would deny Jesus three times. But in the lamplight of the Upper Room earlier at dinner, Peter hadn't believed Him. Did the sound of the rooster crowing bring it all into haunting focus? Did the weight of his own denial, *that Jesus had predicted,* cause him to stop and reflect?

Throughout their relationship, Jesus had left a bread crumb trail, leading Peter on a path to truer understanding of who Jesus really was—and who Peter was *in Him. And this night, is full of breadcrumbs.* Not one thing about this night is a surprise to Jesus. He already knows what each moment would hold.

He'd told Judas he would be the one to betray Him. He'd told the disciples they would all fall away. He'd told Peter that before the rooster crowed three times, he would deny Him. And then, by the light of the charcoal fire, Peter does the very thing Jesus said he would.

Not once. Not twice. *But three times,* Peter is asked, and three times, he denies knowing Jesus. In a matter of hours, Peter had watched as His Rabbi—the one he'd called "the Messiah, the Son of the Living God"—pick up a servant's towel and assume the position of a common slave and wash the disciples' feet. As Judas had led the enemy right to Him, Peter watched as Jesus spoke to Judas saying, "friend, why have you come?" And then Peter had watched as Jesus allowed Himself to be bound and led away.

In his book, *A Fragile Stone,* Michael Card describes the event this way. "Once we have this course of events clearly in mind, we can hear the deeper tone in Peter's denials. *'I do not know the man.'* After all, Peter's Messiah would have slaves washing his feet, not the other way around. His Messiah would command the legions of angels to destroy his enemies. His Messiah would have drawn his own sword as well. Peter understood a king who would take up arms to kill his enemies. Never in his wildest dreams could he imagine a king who would die to save his enemies."[1]

Peter denies Jesus. He denies Him *three times.* Each and every Gospel makes sure that we know this part of the story. But underneath his denial is a current of pain and confusion, and a deep desire for the script to be different. Maybe his mind filled with thoughts like, "No! This isn't how it is supposed to be! He's God! I've seen it with my own eyes! And He's just giving up? I guess He isn't who I thought He was at all. He willingly gave Himself over to be arrested, beaten, and spit on—I don't know *that man* at all."

Luke's Gospel gives us one of the most emotional details of the whole encounter.

> **[60]But Peter was adamant. "Listen, I don't know what you're talking about. Don't you understand? I don't even know him." While the words were still in his mouth, the rooster crowed. [61]At that moment, the Lord, who was being led through the courtyard by his captors, turned around and gazed at Peter. All at once Peter remembered the words Jesus had prophesied over him, "Before the rooster crows in the morning, you will deny three times that you even know me." [62]Peter burst into tears, ran off from the crowd, and wept bitterly. (Luke 22:60-62 TPT)**

As soon as the rooster crows, Jesus looks across the courtyard and into Peter's eyes.

But what Peter sees in the eyes of Jesus is not a look of disappointment. From Jesus, there is no reprimand and no condemnation. Peter has seen this look in the eyes of Jesus before. In fact, the same exact Greek word is used both here in this exchange between Jesus and Peter and also in the *very first exchange* between Jesus and Peter.

The Greek word used to describe the gaze of Jesus is *emblépō.* The exact description is to properly stare or look at with a "locked-in gaze." It means an earnest look that penetrates the heart. It is to look in a sustained, concentrated way, with special "interest, love or concern."[2] Some have said that a more literal translation would be that Jesus "looked *into* Peter."[3]

Even in the heartbreak, Peter sees a familiar gaze from Jesus. The very first time Jesus had looked into Peter's eyes, it was with a look of *emblépō.* We've seen this look before, earlier on this journey at their very first meeting in John 1:42.

When Jesus gazed upon Andrew's brother, he prophesied to him, "You are Simon and your father's name is John. But from now on you will be called Cephas" (which means, Peter the Rock).

That day when they first met, Jesus didn't see Peter through the eyes of what he'd done, then. And on this night, next to the charcoal fire, Jesus doesn't see Peter through the eyes of what he's done now, either.

Just as it has always been, Jesus sees Peter through the lens of His own Covenant and His own love. And this gaze into Peter's eyes—it is a breadcrumb that Jesus is leaving him. Jesus knows Peter well enough to know that *he's broken his own heart* and he'll not quickly recover.

But that's the thing about the loving gaze of Jesus. It wasn't anything that Peter had done that first day they met that compelled Jesus to change his name from Simon to Peter. He'd not yet done anything to prove that he was a rock. But Jesus looked at Peter, as He does all of us, through a filter of His own love and Covenant toward us.

And on this night in the courtyard, next to the charcoal fire, even though Peter's heart is breaking at his own failure, Jesus looks at him the same way. Peter still hasn't done a thing that will cause Jesus to see him through anything less than His own love and Covenant.

Peter runs away weeping bitterly. *He realizes the weight of his sin in the presence of Jesus.* Peter is crushed under the weight of his own denial of the One he'd so fervently pledged he would die for. Peter has broken his own heart and weeps bitterly at the thought of what he's done.

But in the eyes of Jesus, there is only love. The gaze of Jesus holds forgiveness for sin. He sees us not as we are, but as we are *in Him*.

He sees who we really are, in His love, even if we've not behaved as if we are forgiven and set free. When we don't keep our commitment—when we fall short, miss the mark, deny, betray, or walk away from Him—Jesus' gaze toward us remains the same. *He shows us that here.* And it's not because of what we've done, good or bad. *It's entirely because of who He is.* The gaze of Jesus is steady. He sees us through the eyes of a His own love and Covenant with us.

> [38]For I am convinced that neither death, nor life, nor angels, nor principalities, nor things present, nor things to come, nor powers, [39]nor height, nor depth, nor any other created thing, will be able to separate us from the love of God, which is in Christ Jesus our Lord. (Romans 8:38-39 NASB)

VIA DOLOROSA, THE PATH OF JESUS TO THE CROSS

31

²⁷ Then the governor's soldiers took Jesus into the Praetorium and gathered the whole company of soldiers around him. ²⁸ They stripped him and put a scarlet robe on him, ²⁹ and then twisted together a crown of thorns and set it on his head. They put a staff in his right hand. Then they knelt in front of him and mocked him. "Hail, king of the Jews!" they said. ³⁰ They spit on him, and took the staff and struck him on the head again and again. ³¹ After they had mocked him, they took off the robe and put his own clothes on him. Then they led him away to crucify him.

³² As they were going out, they met a man from Cyrene, named Simon, and they forced him to carry the cross. ³³ They came to a place called Golgotha (which means "the place of the skull"). ³⁴ There they offered Jesus wine to drink, mixed with gall; but after tasting it, he refused to drink it. ³⁵ When they had crucified him, they divided up his clothes by casting lots. ³⁶ And sitting down, they kept watch over him there. ³⁷ Above his head they placed the written charge against him: this is jesus, the king of the jews.

³⁸ Two rebels were crucified with him, one on his right and one on his left.³⁹ Those who passed by hurled insults at him, shaking their heads ⁴⁰ and saying, "You who are going to destroy the temple and build it in three days, save yourself! Come down from the cross, if you are the Son of God!" ⁴¹ In the same way the chief priests, the teachers of the law and the elders mocked him. ⁴² "He saved others," they said, "but he can't save himself! He's the king of Israel! Let him come down now from the cross, and we will believe in him. ⁴³ He trusts in God. Let God rescue him now if he wants him, for he said, 'I am the Son of God.'" ⁴⁴ In the same way the rebels who were crucified with him also heaped insults on him.

⁴⁵ From noon until three in the afternoon darkness came over all the land.⁴⁶ About three in the afternoon Jesus cried out in a loud voice, "Eli, Eli, lema sabachthani?" (which means "My God, my God, why have you forsaken me?").

⁴⁷ When some of those standing there heard this, they said, "He's calling Elijah." ⁴⁸ Immediately one of them ran and got a sponge. He filled it with wine vinegar, put it on a staff, and offered it to Jesus to drink. ⁴⁹ The rest said, "Now leave him alone. Let's see if Elijah comes to save him." ⁵⁰ And when Jesus had cried out again in a loud voice, he gave up his spirit.

Matthew 27:27-50 (NIV)

This was the reason Jesus had come. He'd spent His earthly life teaching and preaching, and He'd instituted a New Covenant that abolished the old Law. And now, He's come to pay the ultimate price—to give of His own life as a perfect living sacrifice paid for by His own blood as the atonement for all sin.

Jesus is offering Himself as the final sacrifice—the final perfect Passover Lamb. He is giving His body, the bread, and His blood, the wine, for the ultimate justification of sin. And just like in the garden when He'd been arrested, *Jesus is allowing this to happen.* It's been said that it wasn't the nails that held Jesus to the cross that day, but rather, His love for us. Maybe that has become a cliché statement, but the truth is that *Jesus didn't have to be there at all.* He could have escaped this torturous death in an instant.

Jesus is every bit human as He suffers and agonizes. He thirsts and gasps for breath. His body takes on every bit of treacherous suffering as He hangs there on the cross, bearing the weight of all of the sins of humanity. He could have called on twelve legions of angels to escape that moment and everything it meant. *But instead, He chooses to take on sin and death for you and for me.* The Gospel of Luke paints the picture of Jesus on the cross this way—

> [32] Two other men, both criminals, were also led out with him to be executed. [33] When they came to the place called the Skull, they crucified him there, along with the criminals—one on his right, the other on his left. [34] Jesus said, "Father, forgive them, for they do not know what they are doing." And they divided up his clothes by casting lots. [35] The people stood watching, and the rulers even sneered at him. They said, "He saved others; let him save himself if he is God's Messiah, the Chosen One." [36] The soldiers also came up and mocked him. They offered him wine vinegar [37] and said, "If you are the king of the Jews, save yourself." [38] There was a written notice above him, which read: this is the king of the jews. [39] One of the criminals who hung there hurled insults at him: "Aren't you the Messiah? Save yourself and us!" [40] But the other criminal rebuked him. "Don't you fear God," he said, "since you are under the same sentence? [41] We are punished justly, for we are getting what our deeds deserve. But this man has done nothing wrong." [42] Then he said, "Jesus, remember me when you come into your kingdom." [43] Jesus answered him, "Truly I tell you, today you will be with me in paradise." [44] It was now about noon, and darkness came over the whole land until three in the afternoon, [45] for the sun stopped shining. And the curtain of the temple was torn in two. [46] Jesus called out with a loud voice, "Father, into your hands I commit my spirit." When he had said this, he breathed his last.
> (Luke 23:32-46 NIV)

There is something truly profound that we learn about Jesus in His final exchange on the cross. Those among us who are prone to have a spirit of striving or tallying out our good works before God to please Him should pay close attention to the conversation that Jesus has with the criminal on the cross. The criminal, recognizing his own sin, accepts the just punishment that he deserves, especially in light of the innocence of Jesus on the cross beside him. Their exchange displays such an accurate picture of the gospel of Jesus Christ. The criminal says,

> "Jesus, remember me when you come into your kingdom." Jesus answered him,
> "Truly I tell you, today you will be with me in paradise."

The criminal's eyes are opened and he sees his greatest need. The veil separating the Old and the New is torn. And all at once, Jesus makes a way.

Sincere faith in Jesus as the One who has come to pay for our sins is what reconciles us back to Him. Not a pile of good works or a shiny, perfect faith, but the invitation extended by Jesus to His great Covenant of love. *This criminal only turns from his own sin toward Jesus.* There is not enough time to clean himself up or to impress Jesus with his ability to keep the law in an effort to be made righteous.

There is merely a turning *from himself toward Jesus.* There is simply a new understanding of who Jesus is, and that it is *His* Covenant, not our commitment to Him, that makes it possible for us to be with Him. It is His invitation to meet us where we are, in a posture of humility and repentance in His presence, not our ability to keep the law, become righteous, or obey all of the rules. It is all the work of Jesus on our behalf. His interaction with the criminal on the cross paints a life-changing picture of that for us.

It is the reason He'd come. To seek and to save the lost. And when His time comes, and He willingly steps into the entirety of sin and death out of His great love for us. And Jesus even asks the Father for forgiveness for those who were killing Him. Even in the hour of His greatest suffering, He sees the world that would condemn Him to death, through the lens of His great love. Such mercy. Such grace. Such unimaginable, unmerited favor. This type of love, the world had never known.

> "For God so loved the world, that he gave his only Son, that whoever believes in him should not perish but have eternal life." (John 3:16 ESV)

> "This is how we know what love is: Jesus Christ laid down his life for us." (1 John 3:16 NIV)

CALVARY, GOLGOTHA, THE PLACE OF THE SKULL

32

²⁸After this, when Jesus knew that everything was now finished that the Scripture might be fulfilled, he said, "I'm thirsty." ²⁹A jar full of sour wine was sitting there; so they fixed a sponge full of sour wine on a hyssop branch and held it up to his mouth.

³⁰When Jesus had received the sour wine, he said, "It is finished." Then bowing his head, he gave up his spirit.

John 19:28-30 (CSB)

The words Jesus speaks in His last moments cover the breadth of the gospel and remind us once again why Jesus, Immanuel, God with us, had come.

He said, "It is finished." Then bowing his head, he gave up his spirit.

Jesus is choosing this death. He is choosing to give His life. The original words used here suggest that Jesus bows His head, as one does to bend back and rest, reclining on a pillow. And the words used here to describe how He "gave up His spirit" come from the Greek word meaning *"to yield or to hand over."*[1]

Jesus *gives* His life as an offering. His statement, "it is finished" is translated from the Greek word, *tetelestai*. It means "to bring to an end, to complete, to fulfill," and is the word often used in Biblical times to indicate when a debt had been *"paid in full."*[2] The words Jesus speaks here are an unmistakable reflection of His life, offered as a sacrifice to finish the work, once and for all, to bring all of humanity back to the heart of the Father. His act of completion on the cross pays in full the debt of sin.

Charles Spurgeon says of *tetelestai* that "in the original Greek of John's Gospel, there is only one word for this utterance of our Lord. To translate it into English, we have to use three words; but when it was spoken, it was only one,—an ocean of meaning in a drop of language, a mere drop, for that is all that we can call one word. 'It is finished.' Yet it would need all the other words that ever were spoken, or ever can be spoken, to explain this one word. It is altogether immeasurable."[3]

And deep within the fabric of *the way* the words are woven together is the miraculous covering of the gospel of Jesus Christ. In the original Greek, *tetelestai* is written here in the perfect tense and profoundly indicates both a point in time it was completed and that it would also have the continuing result of being completed or finished.[4] The idea is—"It is finished, *it stands finished*, and it *always will be finished!*" His work of redemption is complete and nothing needs to be or can be added to it.[5]

It is complete. It has been made perfect. The rescue plan which reconciles all God's people back to the Father's heart stands fulfilled. It is finished.

> [9]This is how God showed his love among us: He sent his one and only Son into the world that we might live through him. [10]This is love: not that we loved God, but that he loved us and sent his Son as an atoning sacrifice for our sins… [14]And we have seen and testify that the Father has sent his Son to be the Savior of the world. (1 John 4:9, 10, 14 NIV)

Each Gospel gives us different details about the crucifixion of Jesus. Yet, if we search through all of them, we will find one thing in common. *Peter is nowhere to be found.* When we last saw Peter, he'd just denied Jesus three times and began to weep bitterly. He ran away, undoubtedly crushed by the weight of his own brokenness and failure. The profound irony is, of course, that Jesus is taking on that sin in His greatest act of love and forgiveness.

For Peter, for Judas, for each of the disciples.

For the criminal on the cross next to Him.

For me and for you.

For all of us, for all time, for all eternity.

Jesus chooses to bear the weight of sin, shame, bitterness, selfishness, brokenness, failure, rejection, regret, and inadequacy for generations of people unable to make their way to a Holy God. Jesus chooses to become the way. And He pays for it, in full, with His very life, so that we'd no longer be separated from Him. The cross of Christ has the final word. *It is finished.*

> **For the wages of sin is death, but the free gift of God is eternal life in Christ Jesus our Lord. (Romans 6:23 NIV)**

No longer does the crushing weight of our own sin separate us from the love of Christ. Jesus told us Himself,

> **"The thief comes only to steal and kill and destroy. I came that they may have life
> and have it abundantly." (John 10:10 ESV)**

The disciples have collectively fled in shame, fear, and understandable confusion as Jesus had been arrested, beaten, and then killed. They must be terrified, broken-hearted, and grieving. Their Rabbi and friend had been killed, but what had it all meant?

Like so many of us, they didn't yet see the full picture of God's great story of redemption. And that this story *doesn't end with Jesus on the Cross…it is just the beginning.*

THE GARDEN TOMB

33

¹When the Sabbath was over, Mary Magdalene, and Mary the mother of James, and Salome, bought spices, so that they might come and anoint Him. ²Very early on the first day of the week, they came to the tomb when the sun had risen. ³They were saying to one another, "Who will roll away the stone for us from the entrance of the tomb?" ⁴Looking up, they saw that the stone had been rolled away, although it was extremely large.

⁵Entering the tomb, they saw a young man sitting at the right, wearing a white robe; and they were amazed. ⁶And he said to them, "Do not be amazed; you are looking for Jesus the Nazarene, who has been crucified. He has risen; He is not here; behold, here is the place where they laid Him. ⁷But go, tell His disciples and Peter, 'He is going ahead of you to Galilee; there you will see Him, just as He told you.'"

⁸They went out and fled from the tomb, for trembling and astonishment had gripped them; and they said nothing to anyone, for they were afraid.

Mark 16:1-8 (NASB)

The light on Resurrection morning brings the dawn of a new day. Everything has changed, forevermore. *He has risen; He is not here.*

The grave could not hold Him, and Jesus has conquered sin and death and has risen to new life again!

The power of heaven has shattered the grip of sin, once and for all. Jesus has offered His life in death and has taken it up again with Resurrection power, *just as He said He would.* The ocean between the Crucifixion and the Resurrection brings the echoing invitation to life. His finished work on the cross makes way for all to come and see what God has done. The light of the new day brings the Light of the World, reigning in majesty, alive and sovereign, mighty in power and victorious over death!

He is fully alive and making us alive with Him. Jesus has conquered sin. He has defeated the grave, and now, the empty tomb speaks an eternity's worth of God's unshakeable love. Jesus is alive, and on this Resurrection morning, *He is already about the business of restoration.* His heart is already thinking about those He loves. Did you see it? The heart of Jesus on Resurrection morning is already intentionally reaching out in love.

> **But go, tell His disciples and Peter, "He is going ahead of you to Galilee; there you will see Him, just as He told you."**

Jesus sends a message through the angel waiting at the tomb. Go, and tell the disciples...*and Peter...*

This Savior, in His great love, knows us better than we know ourselves. Jesus knows the heart of Peter well and is already thinking of the moment when Peter hears that He is alive again.

The compassion and intentionality of Jesus here is astounding. He knows that in the hours since He last gazed into his eyes in the courtyard, that Peter has hidden away in shame. And here on Resurrection morning, Jesus is awaiting His reunion with Peter, and those He walked the closest with in life. He is thinking of each of them, and He gives them an invitation.

> **"...Go, tell His disciples and Peter, 'He is going ahead of you to Galilee; there you will see Him, just as He told you.'"**

Jesus is already thinking of them and their restoration, and He extends to them an invitation filled with grace. He is already going before them, just as He'd said, fulfilling His Word, and His Covenant with them, even after each of their own commitments to Him have been found wanting. He wants them to know His great love and will show them by remembering His promise. His invitation is for each of His brothers—the disciples who'd loved and followed Him for the last three years.

But Jesus knows that Peter will feel like he has disqualified himself from this love and this invitation. He speaks to the soul of Peter even in His message.

Go, tell His disciples *and Peter...*It's almost as if Jesus is saying, "take his face in your hands, look into his eyes, and *make sure Peter knows I am inviting him, too.* I know what he's done. And I know what he is feeling. And I want him to know that *I said his name specifically.* Make sure he knows that this invitation is for him, too. I will be waiting for him in Galilee, just as I've said." He'd told them at their Last Supper together...

> **"But after I am raised from the dead, I will go ahead of you to Galilee and meet you there." (Mark 14:28 NLT)**

That night in the Upper Room had that promise even made sense? Had their hearts stopped to take it in then? Jesus had given them a breadcrumb to remember and follow when the time came. Is hope born in them all over again as they hear those familiar words now?

Both grief and fear had crushed the disciples since Jesus had been arrested and killed. We don't know much about the disciples in the days between the Crucifixion and the Resurrection. But we do know that those closest to Jesus are gathered together. They are overcome with grief and quite possibly, terrified for their own safety. They have sequestered themselves together behind closed doors. They are confused by all that has happened. They are grieving the brutal death of their Rabbi and Messiah. And they are facing the reality of the way they fell away in Jesus' greatest hour of need. Many have wondered if Peter would have even allowed himself to be in that gathering of Jesus' closest followers. Or had he been hidden away alone since his weeping had begun that night in the courtyard?

When they hear these words of Jesus, do they dare to believe that His promises are true? Even though He is not yet with them, He is already drawing their hearts back to Himself and pastoring their souls through this grief, fear, and confusion. He'd gone before them once again.

And already, on Resurrection morning, He is going about the business of restoration.

THE GARDEN TOMB

34

⁹When they came back from the tomb, they told all these things to the Eleven and to all the others. ¹⁰It was Mary Magdalene, Joanna, Mary the mother of James, and the others with them who told this to the apostles.

¹¹But they did not believe the women, because their words seemed to them like nonsense.

¹²Peter, however, got up and ran to the tomb. Bending over, he saw the strips of linen lying by themselves, and he went away, wondering to himself what had happened.

Luke 24:9-12 (NIV)

Peter runs. The moment he hears, even though he doesn't understand, he *gets up and runs to the tomb*.

In his shame and his regret, had Peter longed to have one more moment with Jesus? Had he been thinking about what he'd say to Him? Had he been wishing there was a way to turn back time and undo what he'd done? When Peter hears that Jesus might be alive, he runs.

He runs toward Jesus and away from his shame and regret. And what he sees with his own eyes, is that *Jesus is not there*. Had He really risen just as He said?

> **"…He saw the strips of linen lying by themselves, and he went away, wondering to himself what had happened."**

What happens next is a sacred mystery, and something we only know about in part. It appears that Jesus has a moment on Resurrection morning that is similar to many encounters recorded in each of the Gospels, throughout His public ministry. Countless times, we've seen Jesus have a truly life-changing encounter with someone, and then give them instructions to "*go and tell no one*" about it.

And it appears that Jesus has a secret, sacred "go and tell no one" moment with Peter on Resurrection morning. There is only a brief mention of this secret meeting in two places, and nowhere in Scripture do we see recorded what Jesus says to Peter in this personal appearance on Resurrection morning. Because Scripture speaks only briefly and vaguely about this exchange, it might be tempting to give it little weight. But perhaps the fact that little is said about it only further reinforces that it not only takes place, but that it profoundly portrays the heart of Jesus for Peter.

It's mentioned briefly after two men encounter Jesus on the road to Emmaus. When the men realize that the man they'd been walking with had actually been Jesus, they burst in to tell the disciples about it. Only one Gospel mentions it. Luke 24:34 says this—

> **There they found the Eleven and those with them, assembled together and saying, "It is true! The Lord has risen and has appeared to Simon."**

The Lord appears to Simon Peter. Jesus comes to him in a private moment that is for no one else. *It is just for Jesus and Peter.* This side of heaven, we'll never know exactly what Jesus says to Peter in that moment. Perhaps we don't need to know. Maybe it's enough to simply know that one of the first actions of Jesus on Resurrection morning is to seek out Peter to have a moment alone with him. That tells us a lot about Jesus and His love for Peter. The power of sin is great, but the power of Jesus for the forgiveness of sin is greater still.

Peter had come to the tomb that morning to see Jesus, and now Jesus has come to see Peter. We don't know what Jesus says to Peter in those secret moments. But we know the heart of a Savior who wants nothing more than to see those He loves walk in the freedom of the forgiveness He'd just paid for with His own life, death, and now resurrection.

Peter's heart had broken over his own sin. His pride had come before a great fall. But the gaze of Jesus after he'd denied Him showed *a kindness that brought deep repentance* in the heart of Simon Peter. He'd wept bitterly over his own failure. He'd hidden away in shame.

And then, he turns back to Jesus. He runs to him, in fact. Peter becomes a living picture of the very act of repentance—of turning away from sin and back to Jesus.

And though we don't know what Jesus says to Peter that Resurrection morning, it would be easy to imagine that Jesus wants to speak into the heart of Peter that *no sin is too great and no failure too final to separate him from the love of Christ.*

This moment is just between Jesus and Peter. Jesus wants Peter to know that His love for him is unchanged. This moment between the Forgiver and the forgiven, is to make sure that Peter hears that the life-giving message of forgiveness is extended to him too.

Peter will go on to speak about many things, *but he never speaks about this.* He also never speaks directly about his denial again. And neither does Jesus.

Could it be that his encounter with Jesus on this morning, really is a "go and tell no one" moment between them and that Jesus gives Peter instructions to never speak about their encounter or his own failures again? It's possible that the interaction is simply too sacred, too intimate to speak about ever again. It is between Jesus and Peter, and just for the two of them.

The apostle Paul would later reference the secret meeting between Jesus and Peter on Resurrection morning in one of his letters to the Corinthians.

> [3]"...The Messiah died for our sins, exactly as Scripture tells it; [4]that he was buried; that he was raised from death on the third day, again exactly as Scripture says; [5]that he presented himself alive to Peter, then to his closest followers..." (1 Corinthians 15: 3-5 MSG)

There will be more significant moments that happen between Jesus and Peter, but this breadcrumb on the trail cannot be passed over. Soon, the pendulum of these days full of emotion will swing back and give way to that life-changing morning up ahead on the shores at Galilee. The day is soon coming when Jesus will restore Peter and speak to him about his role in the future of the Church. It will be an interaction that will change Peter's life forever.

But *before* Jesus can speak into Peter about *the future*, he needs to speak to Peter's heart about *the past*, and how His forgiveness and grace have the power to change *the present*.

It's a message Jesus is still giving each of us in secret, sacred moments every day. His forgiveness seeks us out, wherever we are, and wherever we've been. And His kindness leads us to repentance. He invites us to come as we are, and His refining love and grace transform us. The invitation is ours to repent and believe, to turn from our own guilt and shame, and to run to Him. And that invitation is not just given on Resurrection Day. But rather, entirely *because of it*.

And it is alive and true today, and every day, for all of us.

VIEW FROM THE EMPTY TOMB

35

¹After the Sabbath, at dawn on the first day of the week, Mary Magdalene and the other Mary went to look at the tomb.

²There was a violent earthquake, for an angel of the Lord came down from heaven and, going to the tomb, rolled back the stone and sat on it. ³His appearance was like lightning, and his clothes were white as snow.

⁴The guards were so afraid of him that they shook and became like dead men.

⁵The angel said to the women, "Do not be afraid, for I know that you are looking for Jesus, who was crucified. ⁶He is not here; he has risen, just as he said. Come and see the place where he lay. ⁷Then go quickly and tell his disciples: 'He has risen from the dead and is going ahead of you into Galilee. There you will see him.' Now I have told you."

⁸So the women hurried away from the tomb, afraid yet filled with joy, and ran to tell his disciples. ⁹Suddenly Jesus met them. "Greetings," he said. They came to him, clasped his feet and worshiped him. ¹⁰Then Jesus said to them, "Do not be afraid. Go and tell my brothers to go to Galilee; there they will see me."

Matthew 28: 1-10 (NIV)

Each Gospel account gives us an incredible look inside all of the life-changing miracles that Resurrection morning holds. The life-altering power of Jesus' victory over death and His miraculous Resurrection is a gift for each and every one of us. It's powerful to see how the Resurrection changes everything. It forever shapes us collectively, as the Body of Christ, and marks us each individually, too.

Jesus has a beautiful life-changing encounter with women dear to His heart that morning there outside the tomb. We know He meets with Peter and the two men on the road to Emmaus, as well. Jesus also thinks of His disciples that morning. Even after following Him closely for three years, they'd all fallen away, just as He'd said they would. And in a stunning act of graciousness, He tells the women,

> "go and tell my brothers to go to Galilee; there they will see me."

Jesus calls them His "*brothers.*" Those aren't the first words that most of us would use to describe trusted, close confidants who'd betrayed and distanced themselves from us in our greatest hour of need. But that is the unexplainable, divine character of God in Jesus. He responds to us, not based on our own commitment to Him, but out of His great Covenant love for us. Even when we feel like we've let Him down. Even when we've given up, stepped away, numbed out, or let fear or peer pressure get the best of us. What some would call "enemies," Jesus calls "*brothers.*"

We can learn so much about Jesus with those few words. And as these brothers—Peter and the other disciples—find themselves still scared to death and unsure of what is happening, and even as they have locked themselves in a room, Jesus comes to them. He comes to them bringing His peace to their fear, their shame, and their confusion. John 20 says this—

> [19] On the evening of that first day of the week, when the disciples were together, with the doors locked for fear of the Jewish leaders, Jesus came and stood among them and said, "Peace be with you!" [20] After he said this, he showed them his hands and side. The disciples were overjoyed when they saw the Lord.
>
> [21] Again Jesus said, "Peace be with you! As the Father has sent me, I am sending you." [22] And with that he breathed on them and said, "Receive the Holy Spirit.
>
> [24] Now Thomas (also known as Didymus), one of the Twelve, was not with the disciples when Jesus came. [25] So the other disciples told him, "We have seen the Lord!" But he said to them, "Unless I see the nail marks in his hands and put my finger where the nails were, and put my hand into his side, I will not believe." [26] A week later his disciples were in the house again, and Thomas was with them. Though the doors were locked, Jesus came and stood among them and said, "Peace be with you!" [27] Then he said to Thomas, "Put your finger here; see my hands. Reach out your hand and put it into my side. Stop doubting and believe." [28] Thomas said to him, "My Lord and my God!" [29] Then Jesus told him, "Because you have seen me, you have believed; blessed are those who have not seen and yet have believed."
>
> [30] Jesus performed many other signs in the presence of his disciples, which are not recorded in this book. [31] But these are written that you may believe that Jesus is the Messiah, the Son of God, and that by believing you may have life in his name.

No matter where we find ourselves today—whether we are hidden away in shame or locked behind a wall of fear, disappointment, or confusion—Jesus is there bringing His peace. Ephesians 2:14 reminds us, "For He Himself is our peace..." Peace is a person—Jesus—and because He is always with us, there can always be rest for our weary souls. Peace is not dependent on our circumstances or our emotions, but as close as our breath.

He seeks us out right in the middle of our hiding. He brings His presence right to our places of doubt. He steps into our lives with His message of forgiveness, covering each of our wounds with His healing touch. He is breathing His Spirit over us, saying, "*Peace be with you.*"

THE GALILEE

36

¹After these things Jesus manifested Himself again to the disciples at the Sea of Tiberias, and He manifested Himself in this way.

²Simon Peter, and Thomas called Didymus, and Nathanael of Cana in Galilee, and the sons of Zebedee, and two others of His disciples were together. ³Simon Peter said to them, "I am going fishing." They said to him, "We will also come with you." They went out and got into the boat; and that night they caught nothing.

⁴But when the day was now breaking, Jesus stood on the beach; yet the disciples did not know that it was Jesus. ⁵So Jesus said to them, "Children, you do not have any fish, do you?" They answered Him, "No." ⁶And He said to them, "Cast the net on the right-hand side of the boat and you will find a catch." So they cast, and then they were not able to haul it in because of the great number of fish.

⁷Therefore that disciple whom Jesus loved said to Peter, "It is the Lord." So when Simon Peter heard that it was the Lord, he put his outer garment on (for he was stripped for work), and threw himself into the sea. ⁸But the other disciples came in the little boat, for they were not far from the land, but about one hundred yards away, dragging the net full of fish.

⁹So when they got out on the land, they saw a charcoal fire already laid and fish placed on it, and bread. ¹⁰Jesus said to them, "Bring some of the fish which you have now caught." ¹¹Simon Peter went up and drew the net to land, full of large fish, a hundred and fifty-three; and although there were so many, the net was not torn.

¹²Jesus said to them, "Come and have breakfast." None of the disciples ventured to question Him, "Who are You?" knowing that it was the Lord. ¹³Jesus came and took the bread and gave it to them, and the fish likewise.

¹⁴This is now the third time that Jesus was manifested to the disciples, after He was raised from the dead.

John 21:1-14 (NASB)

We've been here before. These waters, this rocky shore—it's where it all began. Just like a new year begins and journeys through very different seasons—each with their own beauty and their own ache. And then that same journey leads back to the place it started to begin all over again. There's a poetic irony that Peter and his brothers find their way back to the place where it all began with Jesus—back to the shores of the Sea of Galilee.

These waters, their rocky shores, and the fishing villages that encircle the sea, have been the backdrop for many of the most significant moments of their lives. Three years before, Peter met Jesus for the first time. Simon, the fisherman, had looked into the eyes of the man who would become his Rabbi, Teacher, Messiah, and Friend. And Jesus looked into the eyes of Simon, the fisherman, and called him, Peter, the Rock. And then soon after, on these same rocky shores on the Sea of Galilee, Simon Peter had decided to follow Jesus.

That day on the beach had to have felt like a lifetime ago now. But being back again, Peter must have been thinking of all he'd seen, and heard, and witnessed since that day. Did it feel like those three years had just been a dream? Now here he was again, standing back on the same shore, readying the nets and the boats to fish in the same way that he had for so many years. Even though his eyes would land on familiar sights, on this morning, everything had changed. Nothing was the same.

Peter lived an entire lifetime in those three years walking with Jesus. There had been so much life lived together since that day Peter's eyes were opened to the majesty of the man before him. He'd given everything for the chance to be with Jesus. He'd left behind his work and time with his family for the chance to live, and walk, and learn from Jesus as He brought the gospel of good news. Peter's own life and heart had been changed by the grace, wisdom, humility, authority, and divine power of Jesus.

And now, here they are again. Jesus had told them what would need to happen, but it never made sense. And Peter certainly had thought there could be a better way. But since the last time they'd been fishing, it had all happened, just as Jesus said it would. They'd seen Jesus welcomed with a parade, triumphantly entering Jerusalem to crowds of people calling "save us" to the long-awaited Messiah. But then, it all turned and they saw the shouts of praise turn to cries from an angry mob who called for His death.

What had happened? Where had it all gone wrong? Peter had tried desperately to stop the nightmare unfolding before him, but he'd seen Jesus arrested, beaten, spit on, and flogged. And then his Rabbi, Teacher, Messiah, and Friend put to death on a cross. Three days later, he heard the news that Jesus was raised to life and Peter ran to see for himself. Jesus even came to him in a private, sacred moment after the Resurrection, undoubtedly speaking deep into Peter's heart. Jesus had appeared to their whole group as His disciples and closest followers hid in a locked room, confused, afraid, and unsure. And then He'd come to them again, when Thomas put his hand in the nail holes and they saw for themselves that Jesus really had been raised to new life and stood among them. They'd heard Him speak about a Helper, the Holy Spirit, to guide them. And that morning on the beach they'd never needed it more.

Where is He? Where is Jesus? These days of waiting feel excruciating and endless. What was it all for? How is this God's plan? Back on the shores where his life had been changed, does Peter remember all that Jesus had taught them in their time together? On this morning, Peter's mind must be full of questions. They want to trust His words, but it still doesn't all completely make sense. It must have been bittersweet to be back there again, full circle, where it all began.

But this time, Peter and the disciples are without Jesus. We can all identify with that feeling of believing, but still questioning…following but not sure where the road has taken us. If you've experienced those feelings, you're in good company. And just like Peter and the disciples, even if you don't know exactly where you are on your journey, *Jesus does.* He is with you right where you are, today, and because He is with you, *there is hope.*

Eugene Peterson once said, "hope is a response to the future, which has its foundation in the promises of God. It looks at the future as time for the completion of God's promise. It refuses to extrapolate either desire or anxiety into the future, but instead believes that God's promise gives the proper content to it. But hope is not a doctrine about the future: it is a grace cultivated in the present, it is a stance in the present which deals with the future."[1]

Peter and the disciples may not *feel* hopeful in this moment, back on these shores again. But there is hope set inside them even still, because of the promise of Jesus.

They don't know it yet, but Jesus is coming for them again. And He has something deep in His heart for Peter, the Rock. None of them can sense it quite yet, but the familiar shores of the Sea of Galilee are about to become Holy Ground once more.

DUSK AT GALILEE

37

²Simon Peter, and Thomas called Didymus, and Nathanael of Cana in Galilee, and the sons of Zebedee, and two others of His disciples were together.

³Simon Peter said to them, "I am going fishing." They said to him, "We will also come with you." They went out and got into the boat; and that night they caught nothing.

John 21:2-3 (NASB)

Resurrection day has come and gone. Jesus is alive, and there is good news for the soul of every believer. But what does it look like to follow Jesus in the days *after* the Resurrection? After the dust from the miracle settles, what does it look like to follow Jesus, resurrected in power, but not present, in person?

For these disciples, their faith had been sight. They'd seen with their own eyes Jesus live, and then die, and then raised to new life again. But they are experiencing now what it is, to follow a resurrected Jesus, by faith, *without sight*.

They are the first in the family tree of believers who will wrestle through living out their faith in a Jesus they can feel, but not touch—a Jesus they know, but cannot see. And these disciples are the first to step into a life of learning how to follow Jesus, *even when it feels like He is nowhere to be found.*

Jesus had told the disciples He would meet them in Galilee. *Three times,* in fact, He told them. So without any other clear instructions, they had followed in obedience and traveled back home. Day after day passed, and they longed to hear from Him. To see Him and to have Him make sense of all that they didn't understand. They'd seen Him resurrected with their own eyes, but now, they aren't sure what life is supposed to look like for them. For three years they'd spent each and every day following Jesus, walking with Him, close enough to see the miracles with their own eyes and hear the gospel from His very lips. But what does all of that mean now?

Back on the familiar shores where they'd first followed Him, Peter announces, "I am going fishing." Without any clear direction, Peter goes back to what he knows. Some say that "I'm going fishing" actually means "*I'm going back to fishing.*" Strong's Exhaustive Concordance defines the words used here as meaning to "depart, go away, to lead oneself under, and to withdraw or retire, as if sinking out of sight."[1]

We can't know exactly what is happening deep inside Peter's heart and mind as he decides to pick back up his nets. Is it simply a lack of direction? Is it just a longing for the familiar? For something that feels ordinary and recognizable when nothing else does? Are the disciples still fearing for their lives? Or are they simply hungry and need food or something to live on for a while?

All of these things are possible, and yet there is also a chance there is something deeper going on. Peter had been a zealous and committed follower of Jesus. He'd given his life to it these last few years. But now, Jesus is gone, Peter has denied Him, and *nothing feels like it is supposed to.* Is Peter still wrestling with his own memories? Is he overcome with feelings of failure and shame? Does he feel that his flailing commitment to Jesus at the end now disqualifies him? Is he so crushed and defeated that, in his desperation, he is compelled to turn back to something he *knows* how to do well? He has seen Jesus resurrected, but what is life to look like for a follower, now that there is no one to physically follow?

We can't know all that is playing in the mind of Peter. We only know that on the shores of Galilee, he goes *back to fishing.* And because he is a leader, other disciples follow him.

Have you been there? Regret so thick it feels like it might suffocate you? Maybe you've experienced a failure, or a disappointment, or a loss that threatens to just take you out of the game for good. Or maybe you're at a place where there is no clear direction. And in the absence of a clear vision for the future, you just go back to the last thing that felt good and right.

Or maybe that's not your story at all. Maybe it's not shame, regret, loss, or disappointment that plague you. Maybe it's just that life feels easier and safer when you *go back to what you know.* When the fear of failure creeps close or the disease to please sets in, you convince yourself it's just not worth it. Maybe it's not the feelings of shame or memories of regret that plague you… but instead, the craving for comfort. Maybe it's numbing passivity that keeps you sleep-walking on the sidelines as days fall off the calendar. Maybe it's just easier to stay on auto-pilot, and keep with the old familiar things you've always known, so you never really have to engage with what God has set deep inside you.

We all know what it's like to "go back to fishing." There can be a fine line between doing your best to follow in obedience when there is a no clear direction, and deliberately following at a distance, keeping to the safe and familiar road you've always known.

Part of the mystery of following Christ is just that—it's *full of mystery.* And there is a temptation for each of us to want to *manage the mystery*. When the road ahead is unclear—when we aren't sure what step to take next or what decision to make—it can be tempting, like Peter, to try and "manage the mystery." When we feel out of control, sometimes there is an urge to find what we *can* control. And sometimes, that means returning to something that is not mysterious, but instead, safe and familiar. We often miss what God might have for us simply because we've pulled back, retreated, and tried to sink out of sight from the very thing that feels mysterious. *We all have our own versions of "going back to fishing" in an effort to manage the mystery.*

The thing we forget to remember is that Jesus tells us *He will be with us*. Peter heard Him say it with his own ears. As Jesus appears to the disciples after the Resurrection, He begins to prepare them for moments of mystery, just like this one, with these words in John 14.

> 16"I will ask the Father, and He will give you another Helper, that He may be with you forever; 17that is the Spirit of truth, whom the world cannot receive, because it does not see Him or know Him, but you know Him because He abides with you and will be in you.
>
> 18I will not leave you as orphans; I will come to you. 19After a little while the world will no longer see Me, but you will see Me; because I live, you will live also."

I will be with you. These are the words of Jesus. That promise continues to remind us of God's bigger picture. It can, for all of us, bring a comforting clarity to our souls as we step into the mystery that often comes with following God.

We are reminded again that on this side of the Resurrection, God has already done all the work. Now, He simply invites us to step into all the good works He has already planned in advance for us. We have truth from God's Word to assure us, but sometimes we panic if there is no formula, or no ten easy steps to follow that will guarantee things will all be okay. When we aren't sure which way to walk, we can lift our feet up to take a step in faith anyway, knowing that our feet will land on the rock of His promise. *"I will be with you."*

Every once in a while, we find ourselves in a familiar position—when we don't feel Him, or hear His voice, or know where He'd want us to walk next. And in the absence of knowing exactly what to do, *we are tempted to go just back to fishing*. But with Jesus, there is a clarity to be found *in the mystery*. We can stand firm on the trustworthiness of God. Even when we can't see what's next or don't fully know what following in obedience will look like, we do know that He promises to be right there with us, every step of the way. There is a clarity that only comes in those moments of mystery.

And like Peter, we have a choice. We can try to manage the mystery by "going back to fishing." Or we can take steps of faith into the mystery, believing His promise to be with us. The profound thing is that Jesus meets us right there—right in the middle of the unknown. Jesus comes to meet Peter and the other disciples right where they are. And He does the same with us day after day, bringing new mercies each morning.

He tells us right where to find Him, and He's always waiting there, just as He said He would be. Where is He meeting you today?

CHARCOAL FIRE, SEA OF GALILEE

38

³Simon Peter said to them, "I am going fishing." They said to him, "We will also come with you." They went out and got into the boat; and that night they caught nothing.

⁴But when the day was now breaking, Jesus stood on the beach; yet the disciples did not know that it was Jesus. ⁵So Jesus said to them, "Children, you do not have any fish, do you?" They answered Him, "No." ⁶And He said to them, "Cast the net on the right-hand side of the boat and you will find a catch." So they cast, and then they were not able to haul it in because of the great number of fish. ⁷Therefore that disciple whom Jesus loved said to Peter, "It is the Lord." So when Simon Peter heard that it was the Lord, he put his outer garment on (for he was stripped for work), and threw himself into the sea. ⁸But the other disciples came in the little boat, for they were not far from the land, but about one hundred yards away, dragging the net full of fish.

⁹So when they got out on the land, they saw a charcoal fire already laid and fish placed on it, and bread. ¹⁰Jesus said to them, "Bring some of the fish which you have now caught." ¹¹Simon Peter went up and drew the net to land, full of large fish, a hundred and fifty-three; and although there were so many, the net was not torn.

John 21: 3-11 (NASB)

It is a painfully familiar scene. Another night of fishing and another morning sunrise over empty nets. "*That night they caught nothing.*" They'd been here before. Even a skilled fisherman experiences those days when the fish just aren't biting. And then, another familiar scene begins to unfold. Does it feel like salt in the wound, as someone from the shore begins to call out, asking about their catch?

"Friends, haven't you any fish?"
"No," they answered.

This scene is all too familiar. The bone weariness of a night of fishing with only empty nets to show for it, and then a voice from the shore telling them to cast their nets on the other side of the boat. Something compels them to listen to that voice and throw their nets on the right side, and "*when they did, they were unable to haul the net in because of the large number of fish.*" The miraculous breaks into their ordinary once again. Wait…could it be?

"Then the disciple whom Jesus loved said to Peter, "It is the Lord!""

It's Jesus! The familiar scene comes into focus for all of them. The last time their empty nets were filled to overflowing it had been Jesus, showing them who He was, and now He is showing them again. They hadn't recognized His face or His voice as it carried across the water, but now, there is no mistaking Him. Now they can see the breadcrumbs, and they can't help but follow the trail right back to Him. All night, there had been no fish. But the sound of His voice breaths a miracle, and now the great bounty of fish point their eyes and their hearts back to who is really standing before them. *It is a living and breathing, resurrected Jesus*—their Rabbi and Messiah—revealing to their weary hearts who He really is.

And as if, on cue, Peter is showing us who he is too. The bold and impulsive Peter cannot contain himself. *Once more, Peter is out of the boat.* The sound of Jesus's voice is enough to call him out, and Peter can't wait for the boat to get to shore. He jumps right in, swimming with all his might *toward Jesus.* The boat and the haul of fish behind him, and Jesus before him. Nothing else matters to Peter in that moment.

> [8]But the other disciples came in the little boat, for they were not far from the land, but about one hundred yards away, dragging the net full of fish. [9]So when they got out on the land, they saw a charcoal fire already laid and fish placed on it, and bread.

They say that the sense of smell is the strongest of our senses that is most closely linked to our memories. Incoming smells are actually processed by the areas of the brain that are strongly implicated in emotion and memory. MRI imagery has actually proven the science and brain chemistry behind the way that smells can actually trigger memories from the past.[2]

The moment Peter steps out of the water and onto the shore to approach Jesus, he is met with the smell of the embers burning from *a charcoal fire.* The type of fire that Jesus has set on the beach that morning in this passage comes from the Greek Word, *anthrakia* meaning specifically a "charcoal fire."[3]

There is only one other time that word is used in all of the entire New Testament. It is the same type of fire that Peter was standing beside when he denied Jesus. The smell had to have taken him right back. What is going through Peter's mind as he steps up out of the water in his wet clothes walking toward Jesus, now standing by the charcoal fire?

Jesus comes to the beach that morning to meet Peter right where he is, bringing restoration to every thought, every memory, every fear, and even…*every smell. Only a Savior, full of love and compassion, would be so kind and intentional.*

Their empty nets had been replaced with so many fish that their nets are now full to overflowing. It's peculiar that Scripture tells us it's *153 fish* to be exact. The last time Jesus had given them a miraculous catch the specific amount of fish wasn't mentioned, other than to say that the nets were so full that *they broke*. But this time, John's Gospel takes care to tell us not only the number, but the fact that *the net was not torn under the weight of all 153 fish.*

Biblical historians and commentators have varying opinions on what the number 153 represents. Some say it points to the abundance of God or the completeness of the Trinity, or even the Law and Grace. Some say the numbers represent the Hebrew letters signifying "I AM God." Perhaps most intriguing, is the theory of St. Jerome. It was thought at that time that there were only 153 species of fish in all the world. Meaning, a net full of 153 fish would signify that the invitation to the gospel of Jesus was for all people, and the net, this time unbroken, further signifies this gospel of Jesus extended to all.[4]

What is plain to see here is the invitation of Jesus. He doesn't *need* their fish, which they caught only because of His guidance anyway. Jesus has already provided everything they need for this meal. But in His graciousness, He invites them to bring some of the fish they caught as well.

He is quite literally setting the table for one of the most profound moments of restoration in Scripture. Jesus so intentionally goes before Peter, creating the breadcrumb trail back to Himself, making a way for reconciliation and redemption. With this miraculous catch of fish on the familiar shores of Galilee, right next to a charcoal fire, Jesus is re-creating so many miracles that would speak to Peter's heart.

And if an all-knowing Savior had heard the prayers of a desperate Peter wishing he could go back to that night in the courtyard and do it all over again, then this morning on the shore where it all began, *Jesus will give Peter that very chance.*

DAWN AT THE SEA OF GALILEE

39

¹⁵So when they had finished breakfast, Jesus said to Simon Peter, "Simon, son of John, do you love Me more than these?" He said to Him, "Yes, Lord; You know that I love You." He said to him, "Tend My lambs."

¹⁶He said to him again a second time, "Simon, son of John, do you love Me?" He said to Him, "Yes, Lord; You know that I love You." He said to him, "Shepherd My sheep."

¹⁷He said to him the third time, "Simon, son of John, do you love Me?" Peter was grieved because He said to him the third time, "Do you love Me?" And he said to Him, "Lord, You know all things; You know that I love You." Jesus said to him, "Tend My sheep."

John 21:15-17 (NASB)

What a wonder to behold the gracious Savior who so intentionally pursues those He loves. This Messiah that not only forgives, but also intricately creates a breadcrumb trail leading right to the holy ground of restoration. This miraculous love of a Savior that would so intentionally re-create a moment of shameful wounding, to bring forth the greatest redemption. They are together again, right where it all began. And Jesus gives Peter another invitation. Peter knows well the sound of His Rabbi's voice saying, "Come…" But this morning, the invitation is to breakfast. And while Peter and the others eat the meal that Jesus has prepared, Jesus is also preparing the way for Peter's heart.

Jesus knows well, the heart of this man. His Rock—this impulsive, bold, zealous, honest, authentic, imperfect, and teachable follower that He'd chosen to lead and shepherd His young Church. Jesus had looked right into his eyes that night in the courtyard when Peter's pride and fear had ushered in the crushing blow. Jesus watched as the horror of what Peter had done washed over him, and he began to weep and call down curses on himself. He knew Peter's heart and soul better than even Peter did. Jesus had come to him in a private moment on Resurrection morning, pursuing him with the love and forgiveness that only a rescuing Redeemer could give.

Maybe Peter knew in his heart of hearts that he'd been forgiven. *But did he believe that Jesus still wanted to use him?* Did Peter think he'd disqualified himself from the new name and new mission that Jesus had given him? All we know is that Peter had gone back to fishing. But after a night of catching nothing, Jesus meets him there with a message that would preach His gospel of redemption loud and clear.

The sights are familiar—the rocky, pebbled beach, the boats, and the net. The sounds floating over the water are waves crashing and fishermen, emptying their nets. But the smell—the embers of the charcoal fire fill the air with haunting memories of shame and regret. Over a breakfast of fish and bread, right next to a familiar charcoal fire, Jesus sets the table for a do-over—a true second chance to redeem all that had been lost.

After the meal, Jesus turns His attention squarely on Peter, looks into his eyes, asks him the question—"do you love me?" *Three times,* in fact, he asks the question. *Three times* Jesus gives Peter the chance to shatter the memories of denial he'd been longing to redeem. Scripture says Peter is *grieved* when Jesus asks him the third time. Does he feel like Jesus is asking because his behavior had pointed to the contrary? It must have stirred up so much emotion and broken Peter's heart all over again to hear the question asked again and again.

But Jesus, the Great Physician, is going about the sacred work of healing. Just like a broken bone must be re-set, the treacherous pain of *moving through the brokenness is the only way for true healing to begin.* So Jesus asks the question not once, not twice, but *three times.* "*Simon Peter do you love me?* Each question, covering over the memory of past shame and regret. Each answer, moving a step closer to true restoration. Each of the three questions, offering an opportunity to replace the haunting memory of denial with a renewed and redeemed confession of love.

This interaction is significant in every way, but in our English translation, we miss the great depth and power of what is really going on underneath. The original language of the carefully chosen words being used that day over the firelight paint a picture of the true Covenant love of Jesus, and they are worth a closer look. As is so often the case, there is a profound theology lesson tucked inside the grammar of what is really being said.

"Love" is a word that can mean so many things. In English, you can use the same word--"love"—to describe your feelings about the weather, ice cream, new shoes, Christmas morning, your grandmother, and your soul mate. The same word can be found in a children's book, a country song, or marriage vows. To us, and especially in English, the word "love" can be a word that literally covers a multitude of things.

In Greek, however, there are separate words used to describe different kinds of love. Each word speaks to exactly the type of love being given and received. When Jesus asks Peter the question, the first two times, He phrases the question using an *agapaó* type of love, and all three times Peter responds using a *phileó* type of love. In the Greek, to love with *agapé* love is to love, value, esteem, be faithful towards and delight in. In the New Testament, this type of love is the love of God for

His Son and His people, and the active love His people are to have for God, each other and even enemies.[1]

To love with a *phileō* type of love is to show tender affection in intimate friendship, characterized by warm, heartfelt consideration and kinship.[2] The contrast magnifies that a biblical definition of love *begins with God, never with us.* God's character defines love, and He seeks and saves an undeserving world with His unconditional, pure, and perfect *agape* love.[3] Their exchange is meaningful as we read it in English, but there is profound, life-changing power in these words spoken in the original language. With the reflection of firelight in His eyes, Jesus looks at Peter, with the all-knowing eyes of a Savior's love.

"Simon, son of John, do you love *(agapas)* me?" Peter says, "yes, Lord, you know that I love *(philō)* you." And a second time Jesus asks, "Simon, son of John, do you love *(agapas)* Me?" And Peter replies, "yes Lord, you know that I love *(philō)* you." And then Jesus said to him the third time, "Simon, son of John, do you love *(phileis)* Me?" Peter was grieved because He said to him the third time, "Do you love *(phileis)* Me?" And Peter said to Him, "Lord, You know all things; You know that I love *(philō)* You."

The original language paints the picture of the breadcrumb trail that Jesus has been leaving back to Himself all along. Jesus knows that Peter can't say, "Jesus, I love you, in the same way that you love me." Only Jesus is capable of that kind of love. And that realization, made in a posture of humility and surrender, brings life-giving freedom for Peter and for all of us. Although deep, the love that ushers in our commitment to Jesus is still imperfect. But it is also covered over by the complete and perfect unconditional Covenant love that Jesus has for us first.

There is a sense here that Jesus wants Peter to see with eyes wide open that, even though his own love and commitment to Jesus may fail, or falter, or come up short, the perfect and complete *agape* love of Jesus covers over it. Jesus is not surprised when even our most selfless and noble efforts to love Him fall short. In fact, it is Jesus who is making the distinction between His love and ours. And Jesus preaches a message of redemption and restoration that will speak deep into the heart and soul of Peter. After His invitation to breakfast, Jesus fully restores Peter, and then sends him out with these words—*"follow me."*

> [18]"Truly, truly, I say to you, when you were younger, you used to gird yourself and walk wherever you wished; when you grow old, you will stretch out your hands and someone else will gird you, and bring you where you do not wish to go." [19]Now this He said, signifying by what kind of death he would glorify God. And when He had spoken this, He said to him, "Follow Me!" [20]Peter, turning around, saw the disciple whom Jesus loved following them; the one who also had leaned back on His bosom at the supper and said, "Lord, who is the one who betrays You?" [21]So Peter seeing him said to Jesus, "Lord, and what about this man?" [22]Jesus said to him, "If I want him to remain until I come, what is that to you? You follow Me!" (John 21:18-22 NASB)

"Follow me…" Jesus speaks about future suffering that is part of the road in the cause of Christ, and when Peter begins to compare himself with John, on both occasions, the words of Jesus are simply *"follow me."* In his book, *As Kingfishers Catch Fire*, Eugene Peterson said that this "story involves Jesus's insistence that Peter's place in the kingdom is to maintain his self-awareness as Jesus's follower (not leader) in the Christian community. The Christian life does not consist in achieving great things for God but in allowing Jesus to use our inadequacy and failure to rehabilitate us to a life experienced as grace and love and obedience. Peter's recovered focus on following Jesus to a sacrificial death, undistracted by what others might or might not be doing under Jesus's emphatic 'Follow me,' is basic for each of us. The Christian life is not about leadership but 'followership,' not about becoming more and more but less and less."[4]

With this final exchange in John 21, it's almost as if Jesus wants Peter to hear His heart saying,

"Simon Peter, I know exactly who you are. I know who you have always been, and I know who you will be. I know that your heart longs to love me with a love that never fails, but only I can love that way. I am not surprised when your love and commitment fall short. My love covers over the gaps, and my Covenant with you reaches all the way from My heart to yours. I know you will fall. I know you will make mistakes. I know you will step out of the boat and sink. *And I still choose you. Follow Me.* I will love with an everlasting love that is perfect, and unconditional, and has already made a way. I have come to bring life—to rescue, redeem, and restore. And in response to all that I've already done, I give you the invitation to care for all the sheep still wandering without a Shepherd. *Lead them by following Me.* From the back, you'll look like a shepherd the flock can follow, but from the front, you'll look like a sheep in My flock. And as I shepherd you, follow Me.[5.] You've been Simon, and now you are Peter. You've been a fisherman, and now you are a fisher of men. You'll become a shepherd of my flock, *but you'll never stop being a sheep as you follow Me*, the Good Shepherd. I am the Cornerstone, but you are My Rock, and I still choose you to shepherd and care for My people. Teach them, care for them, feed them My Word. I've left you the breadcrumb trail that always leads you back to Me. There is nothing that can separate you from My great love, and there is no failure that disqualifies you from loving My people and joining me in building My Church. My Covenant with you has made the way. *Follow me...*"

So there on the beach, next to the charcoal fire, Jesus is making all things new again. True redemption and full restoration are found deep within the Covenant love of Jesus. *For Peter, for you, and for all of us.*

SUNRISE AT THE SEA OF GALILEE

40

¹After these things Jesus manifested Himself again to the disciples at the Sea of Tiberias, and He manifested Himself in this way. ²Simon Peter, and Thomas called Didymus, and Nathanael of Cana in Galilee, and the sons of Zebedee, and two others of His disciples were together. ³Simon Peter said to them, "I am going fishing." They said to him, "We will also come with you." They went out and got into the boat; and that night they caught nothing.

⁴But when the day was now breaking, Jesus stood on the beach; yet the disciples did not know that it was Jesus. ⁵So Jesus said to them, "Children, you do not have any fish, do you?" They answered Him, "No." ⁶And He said to them, "Cast the net on the right-hand side of the boat and you will find a catch." So they cast, and then they were not able to haul it in because of the great number of fish. ⁷Therefore that disciple whom Jesus loved said to Peter, "It is the Lord." So when Simon Peter heard that it was the Lord, he put his outer garment on (for he was stripped for work), and threw himself into the sea. ⁸But the other disciples came in the little boat, for they were not far from the land, but about one hundred yards away, dragging the net full of fish.

⁹So when they got out on the land, they saw a charcoal fire already laid and fish placed on it, and bread. ¹⁰Jesus said to them, "Bring some of the fish which you have now caught." ¹¹Simon Peter went up and drew the net to land, full of large fish, a hundred and fifty-three; and although there were so many, the net was not torn.

¹²Jesus said to them, "Come and have breakfast." None of the disciples ventured to question Him, "Who are You?" knowing that it was the Lord. ¹³Jesus came and took the bread and gave it to them, and the fish likewise. ¹⁴This is now the third time that Jesus was manifested to the disciples, after He was raised from the dead.

¹⁵So when they had finished breakfast, Jesus said to Simon Peter, "Simon, son of John, do you love Me more than these?" He said to Him, "Yes, Lord; You know that I love You." He said to him,

"Tend My lambs." [16]He said to him again a second time, "Simon, son of John, do you love Me?" He said to Him, "Yes, Lord; You know that I love You." He said to him, "Shepherd My sheep." [17]He said to him the third time, "Simon, son of John, do you love Me?" Peter was grieved because He said to him the third time, "Do you love Me?" And he said to Him, "Lord, You know all things; You know that I love You." Jesus said to him, "Tend My sheep.

[18]Truly, truly, I say to you, when you were younger, you used to gird yourself and walk wherever you wished; but when you grow old, you will stretch out your hands and someone else will gird you, and bring you where you do not wish to go." [19]Now this He said, signifying by what kind of death he would glorify God. And when He had spoken this, He said to him, "Follow Me!"

[20]Peter, turning around, saw the disciple whom Jesus loved following them; the one who also had leaned back on His bosom at the supper and said, "Lord, who is the one who betrays You?" [21]So Peter seeing him said to Jesus, "Lord, and what about this man?" [22]Jesus said to him, "If I want him to remain until I come, what is that to you? You follow Me!" [23]Therefore this saying went out among the brethren that that disciple would not die; yet Jesus did not say to him that he would not die, but only, "If I want him to remain until I come, what is that to you?"

[24]This is the disciple who is testifying to these things and wrote these things, and we know that his testimony is true.

[25]And there are also many other things which Jesus did, which if they were written in detail, I suppose that even the world itself would not contain the books that would be written.

John 21: 1-25 (NASB)

And so it was…The First Breakfast. After three years together, it wasn't the first invitation Jesus gave to Peter, but in so many ways, it was the most life-changing. *"Come and have breakfast…"*

The pastel morning sky painted the backdrop over the pebbled beach. The waves at the shore of the Sea of Galilee swayed back and forth, steady like a heartbeat. The crackle of the campfire floated over the water. The breeze was fresh with the aroma of the sea and a breakfast of fish and bread. The early morning sun would soon rise up over the hills in the distance, beckoning not just a new day, but new mercies brought to life by the very sound of His voice.

"Come and have breakfast." They don't sound like the kinds of words that could change a life forever. It's an everyday, ordinary sort of invitation. You might have even uttered those words yourself, standing bleary-eyed in your kitchen, this morning.

But on this unforgettable morning, the air became thick with the life-altering possibility of redemption. Like when a storm rolls in, the air changed, the wind shifted, and the dark pebbled beach became sacred holy ground. This was no ordinary invitation to breakfast.

Burned in Peter's memory, were all the things that came to pass on the night of *The Last Supper.* Memories of denial, shame, guilt, inadequacy, fear, and regret. But this morning, filled with its new mercies and an invitation to redemption…this would become *The First Breakfast.*

Those words of Jesus—*"Come and have breakfast—"* became a melody to drown out the shame and regret. This invitation was a single moment, suspended in time, intentionally crafted by an all-knowing Savior, whose heart beats for restoration.

After three years, this moment is the crescendo in the life-changing story of Jesus and Peter. With all its sights, and sounds, and smells, it paints the picture of how the saving love of Jesus covers over paralyzing shame, heartbreaking inadequacy, and the messiness of human brokenness.

It is the story of the reckless love of a Savior, chasing after an imperfect, flailing believer. It is the story of Jesus and Peter. But it is, just as much, *the story of us.*

You and I. We too have felt the pursuit of His love and the gracious hand of His forgiveness. But we've also known the heartbreaking regret of our own mistakes, the pain of our own sin, and the brokenness of not measuring up. So, this sweeping cinematic story of the ever-turning, winding relationship of Jesus and Peter, we need to let it soak in and change us. We've seen the heights of supernatural, Spirit-filled wisdom and faith and also the plummeting depths of failure and shame. And we've seen the relentless pursuit of a Savior, whose Covenant love crushes fear, doubt, shame, passivity, resignation, and brokenness.

This story of *Jesus and Peter*—it is very much the story of *the Father and us.* It gives us the most beautiful picture of the limitless grace of our rescuing Redeemer. And it helps us to understand how He chooses and chases after the messy and broken ones He loves. And perhaps even more importantly, it teaches us *who we are*, in the eyes of a Savior, who emptied out His whole life for our very own. The words Jesus spoke to Peter on the beach that day were a simple invitation that changed everything.

They are a song of redemption—

For Peter.

For you.

For all of us.

This journey of Jesus and Peter is a true story. The question is, of course, *has it become true for you?* Can you see yourself the way Jesus sees you? Will you answer the invitation He gives you each day to "come and have breakfast?"

The whispers that tempt you to believe the lies that you've strayed too far, or that He'd never use you…those lies are silenced by the sound of His voice that brings new mercy each morning.

The First Breakfast is an invitation to Peter and to all of us. Today and tomorrow, and for all of the days that are yet to come.

His Covenant is greater than our commitment.

And within His invitation, there are messages of rest, redemption, restoration, and hope that echo over us…

I still choose you.

You have not let me down.
You are not too much.
You have not strayed too far.
Your life can still speak of my unfailing love.
You will make mistakes, but I am with you.
Even in all your brokenness, I am still reaching out My hand to you.
In all the ways you may try and fail, I will refine you with the Father's love.
I will carry you. I will rescue you. I will redeem you, and I will bring you rest.
I love you. I forgive you. I still choose you, and I am with you, always.
Follow Me.
Come and have breakfast.

GALILEE AT DAWN

EPILOGUE

Peter would go on to live out his true calling from a place of rest and restoration. His journey with Jesus through calling, brokenness, and restoration transformed him from Simon, the fisherman, into Peter, the Rock. He went on to rise up to the name and calling Jesus had given him the very first day they met.

The First Breakfast was not the end of Peter's story. In so many ways, it was just the beginning. Peter went on to live several more decades, and those years could have looked entirely different if it hadn't been for the pursuit of Jesus. Three years in the presence of Jesus, following closely as a disciple had transformed Peter. But it was their morning on the shores of the Sea of Galilee that charted Peter's course for the rest of his days.

The First Breakfast changed everything. Jesus had always known who Peter could become. But maybe Peter had to travel the breadcrumb trail through the messy middle of transformation. That journey led him to the beach that morning so that he could see for himself, through the eyes of Jesus, who he really was.

For us too, it can be a journey to finally believe for ourselves, that we are who Jesus says that we are. It is an invitation that Jesus gives to each of us. It's one thing to answer His call and to follow Him, but it's another thing entirely to be transformed by His Covenant love that is greater than our commitment. Only when we believe His words and begin to see ourselves as He sees us, can we live out our calling as followers from a place of true rest and full restoration.

The breadcrumb trail is there for us, too. And we can follow Him there every morning as He invites us to "*come and have breakfast.*"

Many things have been said about Peter, but perhaps none more profound than the words used to describe him in the book of Acts. Peter, alongside his close friend John, begins to shepherd the young new Church, and he stands before the authorities to defend the cause of Christ. Acts 4:13 (NLT) says this—

> The members of the council were amazed when they saw the boldness of Peter and John, for they could see that they were ordinary men with no special training in the Scriptures. They also recognized them as men who had been with Jesus.

Peter's time in the presence of Jesus had so transformed him that when he spoke, people could tell *he had been with Jesus.* Simon, the fisherman was transformed into Peter, the Rock, in every way. Jesus told Peter who he really was. In time, Peter was able to make his own confession of Christ by telling Jesus that he knew who He really was. And Peter would go on to tell us who we really are, as well, in his letters to believers in the Church. The life-changing gift of *time with Jesus* is undeniably evident in the writing of Peter. Only a man *truly transformed by the presence of Jesus* would go on to give us these life-changing words–

> ³Blessed be the God and Father of our Lord Jesus Christ. Because of his great mercy he has given us new birth into a living hope through the resurrection of Jesus Christ from the dead ⁴and into an inheritance that is imperishable, undefiled, and unfading, kept in heaven for you. ⁵You are being guarded by God's power through faith for a salvation that is ready to be revealed in the last time. ⁶You rejoice in this, even though now for a short time, if necessary, you suffer grief in various trials ⁷so that the proven character of your faith—more valuable than gold which, though perishable, is refined by fire—may result in praise, glory, and honor at the revelation of Jesus Christ. ⁸Though you have not seen

him, you love him; though not seeing him now, you believe in him, and you rejoice with inexpressible and glorious joy, ⁹because you are receiving the goal of your faith, the salvation of your souls. (I Peter 1:3-9 CSB)

¹¹If anyone speaks, they should do so as one who speaks the very words of God. If anyone serves, they should do so with the strength God provides, so that in all things God may be praised through Jesus Christ. To him be the glory and the power for ever and ever. (1 Peter 4:11 NIV)

¹⁵But in your hearts revere Christ as Lord. Always be prepared to give an answer to everyone who asks you to give the reason for the hope that you have. But do this with gentleness and respect. (1 Peter 3:15 NIV)

⁹But you are a chosen people, a royal priesthood, a holy nation, God's special possession, that you may declare the praises of him who called you out of darkness into his wonderful light. (1 Peter 2:9 NIV)

²⁴He Himself bore our sins in His body on the cross, so that we might die to sin and live to righteousness; for by His wounds you were healed. (1 Peter 2:24 NASB)

⁹The Lord is not slow to fulfill his promise as some count slowness, but is patient toward you, not wishing that any should perish, but that all should reach repentance. (2 Peter 3:9 ESV)

³His divine power has given us everything we need for a godly life through our knowledge of him who called us by his own glory and goodness. ⁴Through these he has given us his very great and precious promises, so that through them you may participate in the divine nature, having escaped the corruption in the world caused by evil desires. ⁵For this very reason, make every effort to add to your faith goodness; and to goodness, knowledge; ⁶and to knowledge, self-control; and to self-control, perseverance; and to perseverance, godliness; ⁷and to godliness, mutual affection; and to mutual affection, love. ⁸For if you possess these qualities in increasing measure, they will keep you from being ineffective and unproductive in your knowledge of our Lord Jesus Christ. ⁹But whoever does not have them is nearsighted and blind, forgetting that they have been cleansed from their past sins. ¹⁰Therefore, my brothers and sisters, make every effort to confirm your calling and election. For if you do these things, you will never stumble, ¹¹and you will receive a rich welcome into the eternal kingdom of our Lord and Savior Jesus Christ. (2 Peter 1:3-11 NIV)

The First Breakfast set Peter on a new path. The forgiveness of Christ drew Peter to move through the darkness of his brokenness, and into the bright light of peace and freedom in the Covenant love of Jesus. There was purpose in Peter's season of brokenness that led him on a journey of spiritual formation and gave him eyes to see his need for Christ, as well as his place in God's redemption story. The way that Peter lives out the rest of his days shows us how true that can be for all of us. Now we've seen up close and can recognize that process of weathering—how a rock is smoothed, softened, and changed by water over time. In the same way, the journey of Simon the fisherman to becoming Peter the Rock, confirms that being in the presence of Jesus truly is the most transforming force the world has ever known. Fully forgiven, and fully restored, Peter went on to live out his calling and mission by freely giving his life away, as Christ had first given His.

The story of Jesus and Peter reminds us too, that as followers of Jesus we are forgiven and set free. And we also remember that we too, are called to give our lives away for the glory of God and the good of others. The gift of restoration in Jesus means that He is with us, and He takes us by the hand and leads us down the narrow road.

The First Breakfast, and the story of Jesus and Peter is an invitation to see more clearly the Father's heart for us, and how He pursues us even in our brokenness, transforming us in His presence. When we respond to His invitation, we can see more clearly who we are in Him, and in His Covenant love that is so much greater than our commitment to Him. And then, from that place of true rest and full restoration, we can live out our calling as Christ's followers, forgiven and set free.

So, as we continue our journey, this is our prayer—
Jesus, may this be true of us, too.
May we give ourselves and our brokenness, as an offering to be transformed in Your presence.
Give us eyes to see ourselves the way You see us.
May we live forgiven and free in Your Covenant Love,
as we follow You down the narrow road that leads to life.
May we live out our calling as followers from a place of true rest and full restoration.
And may we answer the invitation that You give to us each day to "come and have breakfast…"

ENDNOTES

Prologue
1. https://www.biblestudytools.com/dictionary/manna/

01
1. Ray Vander Laan, That the World May Know Ministries; https://www.thattheworldmayknow.com/the-sea-of-galilee
2. https://www.drivethruhistory.com/sea-of-galilee/
3. http://www.biblearchaeology.org/post/2009/03/Jesus-and-the-Sea-of-Galilee.aspx#Article
4. Ray Vander Laan, That the World May Know Ministries; https://www.thattheworldmayknow.com/to-be-a-talmid
5. https://www.nationalgeographic.org/encyclopedia/weathering/

02
1. Jeremiah 29:13,14 (ESV)
2. Ray Vander Laan, That the World May Know Ministries; https://www.thattheworldmayknow.com/to-be-a-talmid

03
1. https://biblehub.com/greek/1689.htm, HELPS Word-studies
2. Schaff, Philip. "Commentary on John 1:42" *Schaff's Popular Commentary on the New Testament* https:https://www.studylight.org/commentaries/scn/john-1.html. 1879-90.
3. https://www.michelangelo.org/michelangelo-quotes.jsp

04
1. Inspired by words from Michael Card, *A Fragile Stone: the emotional life of Simon Peter* (InterVarsity Press, Downers Grove, IL, 2003), 41

06
1. https://www.biblicalarchaeology.org/daily/biblical-sites-places/biblical-archaeology-sites/the-house-of-peter-the-home-of-jesus-in-capernaum/
2. Strong's NT 2008 ; https://biblehub.com/greek/2008.htm
3. https://biblehub.com/greek/2008.htm, HELPS Word-studies
4. https://www.biblegateway.com/verse/EN/Psalm+18:35

08
1. https://www.goodreads.com/quotes/44447-the-great-thing-if-one-can-is-to-stop-regarding

09
1. Ray Vander Laan, That the World May Know Ministries; https://www.thattheworldmayknow.com/sea-of-galilee-geography
2. Strong's NT 928; https://biblehub.com/greek/928.htm

12
1. Ray Vander Laan, That the World May Know Ministries; https://www.thattheworldmayknow.com/gates-of-hell
2. https://www.focusonthefamily.com/socialissues/sexuality/christianity-and-cultural-change/christ-challenges-the-disciples-take-the-gospel-to-the-gates-of-hell

14
1. Dr. Larry Crabb, *When God's Ways Make No Sense* (Grand Rapids, MI: Baker Publishing Group, 2018), 95, 22

<u>15</u>
1.https://biblehub.com/sermons/auth/body/the_mountain_where_the_transfiguration_took_place.htm
2.https://www.bibletools.org/index.cfm/fuseaction/Topical.show/RTD/cgg/ID/2529/Law-Prophets.htm
3. https://biblehub.com/greek/3339.htm

<u>17</u>
1.http://www.crivoice.org/seder.html

<u>18</u>
1. *Christ in the Passover*, pamphlet (Rose Publishing, Carson, California, 2008)

<u>19</u>
1. Barney Kasdan, *God's Appointed Times; a Practical Guide for Understanding and Celebrating the Biblical Holidays*, (Messianic Jewish Publishers, Baltimore, MD, 1993), 27.

<u>20</u>
1. Michael Card, *A Fragile Stone: the emotional life of Simon Peter* (InterVarsity Press, Downers Grove, IL, 2003), 88,89

<u>21</u>
1. https://biblehub.com/commentaries/luke/22-31.htm / Meyer's NT Commentary
2. Strong's NT 1809; https://biblehub.com/greek/1809.htm
3. https://biblehub.com/interlinear/luke/22-31.htm, https://biblehub.com/interlinear/luke/22-32.htm
4. https://www.biblestudytools.com/commentaries/gills-exposition-of-the-bible/luke-22-31.html

<u>22</u>
1. https://www.biblestudytools.com/dictionary/hallel/
2. Matthew 26:30, Complete Jewish Bible
3. https://www.biblestudytools.com/encyclopedias/isbe/hallelujah.html
4. https://biblehub.com/library/spurgeon/till_he_come/the_memorable_hymn_and_when.htm
5. Israel Institute for Biblical Studies, https://www.youtube.com/watch?v=HNnlHeNOr8A
6. Strong's OT 3444; https://biblehub.com/hebrew/3444.htm
7.https://jewsforjesus.org/publications/newsletter/newsletter-dec-1987/y-shua-the-jewish-word-for-salvation/

<u>23</u>
1.http://www.searchingthescriptures.net/main_pages/articles/portraits_of_jesus/portraits_of_jesus_2.htm

<u>26</u>
1.The True Vine Meditations for a Month on John 15:1-16 by Rev. Andrew Murray 1828-1917
2. Strong's NT 3306; https://biblehub.com/greek/3306.htm

<u>27</u>
1.https://www.biblestudytools.com/dictionary/gethsemane/,https://biblehub.com/greek/1068.htm
2. Ray Vander Laan, That the World May Know Ministries; https://www.thattheworldmayknow.com/gethsemane-and-the-olive-press
3. Strong's NT 4561; https://biblehub.com/greek/4561.htm

<u>28</u>
1. Strong's NT 4686; https://biblehub.com/greek/4686.htm

2. https://renner.org/how-many-soldiers-does-it-take-to-arrest-one-man/
3. Strong's NT 4098; https://biblehub.com/greek/4098.htm
4. Strong's NT 3162; https://biblehub.com/greek/3162.htm

29

1. https://www.studylight.org/commentaries/dsb/john-18.html

30

1.Michael Card, *A Fragile Stone: the emotional life of Simon Peter* (InterVarsity Press, Downers Grove, IL, 2003), 110
2.Strong's NT 1689; https://biblehub.com/greek/1689.htm
3. http://christadelphianbooks.org/haw/word_studies/ch11.html

32

1.Strong's NT 1689; https://biblehub.com/greek/1689.htm
2.Strong's NT 5055; https://biblehub.com/greek/5055.htm
3.Charles Spurgeon's Writings- Christ's Dying Word for His Church. January 21st, 1894, Metropolitan Tabernacle, Newington
4.The Hebrew-Greek Key Word Study Bible, New American Standard Bible (AMG Publishers, Chattanooga, TN, 1990) Grammatical Notations, 1703
5.https://www.blueletterbible.org/help/lexicalDefinitions.cfm?lang=G&num=5778, https://www.blueletterbible.org/help/greekverbs.cfm

36

1.Eugene H. Peterson, *Like Dew Your Youth: Growing Up with Your Teenager* (Grand Rapids, Michigan: William B. Eerdmans Publishing Company, 1998), 72,73

37

1. Strong's NT 5217; https://biblehub.com/greek/5217.htm

38

1.https://biblehub.com/commentaries/john/21-5.htm, Expositor's Greek Testament
2. https://www.psychologytoday.com/us/blog/brain-babble/201501/smells-ring-bells-how-smell-triggers-memories-and-emotions
3. Strong's NT 438; https://biblehub.com/greek/439.htm
4. https://bible.org/seriespage/john-21

39

1. https://www.billmounce.com/greek-dictionary/agapao
2. Strong's NT 5368; https://biblehub.com/greek/5368.htm
3. https://www.thegospelcoalition.org/article/love-does-not-begin-with-you/
4. Eugene H. Peterson, *As kingfishers catch fire : a conversation on the ways of God formed by the words of God* (Colorado Springs, Colorado: WaterBrook, 2017), 357
5. Inspired by words from W. Phillip Keller, *A Shepherd Looks at Psalm 23* (Grand Rapids, Michigan: Zondervan, 1970)

The images included here are not meant to confirm exact locations of encounters in Scripture, but rather to bring inspiration and understanding from the general areas and events mentioned in the corresponding passages.

MEET THE AUTHORS

Eric and Kristin Hill began With You Ministries in 2010, with a vision and mission to create resources and experiences to help you rest and remember that God is with you. Eric is an ordained pastor, and communicator, certified in Soul Care and spiritual direction, and Kristin is a writer and Bible teacher. Since 1996 they have had the privilege of leading together and serving individuals, students, parents, and families, in various positions within the church, camp, school, and business settings. They are passionate about creating Christ-centered experiences and resources that help you live from a place of rest. They wake up every day, grateful for the opportunity and privilege to follow Jesus and walk with each other and with you.

Eric and Kristin live in Milton, Georgia and have three beautiful daughters.

To learn more or connect with Eric and Kristin, visit www.withyouministries.com.

Also available from With You Ministries—
Go and Tell No One | Remember and Rest in the Secret and the Sacred, a Six-Week Bible Study from Kristin Hill

MEET THE PHOTOGRAPHER

Hannah Elizabeth Taylor is a lover of Christ, a daughter, a sister, a friend, and an international photojournalist. The closer she walks with the Great Storyteller Himself, the quicker her heart beats to unearth His fingerprints throughout creation. Hannah comes alive when she is able to celebrate and champion people, places and cultures through the art of visual storytelling.

To keep up with her adventures and stories along the way, visit www.hannahelizabethstories.com.

CPSIA information can be obtained
at www.ICGtesting.com
Printed in the USA
LVHW070839150819
627695LV00001B/1/P